Receiving Woman

Published by The Westminster Press

BOOKS BY ANN AND BARRY ULANOV

Cinderella and Her Sisters:
The Envied and the Envying

Religion and the Unconscious

BOOK BY ANN BELFORD ULANOV

Receiving Woman:
*Studies in the Psychology and Theology
of the Feminine*

Published by Northwestern University Press

BOOK BY ANN BELFORD ULANOV

The Feminine in Jungian Psychology
and in Christian Theology

Published by John Knox Press

BOOK BY ANN AND BARRY ULANOV

Primary Speech:
A Psychology of Prayer

RECEIVING WOMAN

Studies in the Psychology
and Theology
of the Feminine

by

ANN BELFORD ULANOV

The Westminster Press
Philadelphia

Book Design by Alice Derr

Published by The Westminster Press®
Philadelphia, Pennsylvania

PRINTED IN THE UNITED STATES OF AMERICA
9 8 7 6 5 4 3

Library of Congress Cataloging in Publication Data

Ulanov, Ann Belford.
    Recieving woman.

    Includes bibliographical references.
    1. Women—Psychology. 2.   Identity (Psychology)
3. Sex discrimination against women. 4.   Woman
(Christian theology) I.   Title.
HQ1206.U48   305.4'2   80–26813
ISBN 0–664–24360–6

For Barry

Contents

Preface   11

1. Receiving Woman   15

2. Detours to Dead Ends   33

3. Relocating the Issue   53

4. Receiving the Feminine Elements of Being   72

5. The Birth of Otherness: The Feminine Elements of
   Being and the Religious Life   90

6. The Authority of Women   115

7. Woman Receiving   149

Notes   179

Preface

This book is composed of a series of studies on a common theme and set of concerns. The subject is woman's psychology and special role in religion. It leads into a consideration of the feminine aspects of personality and their bearing on belief in God. The chapters come together around a central conviction: that a woman consenting to be all of herself brings into the world a quality of consciousness and spirit we all need very much. In these times of agitation concerning women's rights, it is easy to forget the force of the quality of life of particular women, and the presence each brings in her own way to our shared life together. That is the focus of this book.

Many of the insights for these chapters came out of discussion in class and conference with my women students, and I thank them warmly for their contribution to my understanding. In addition, the women I have worked with in analysis have given me many insights into the rich differences among women and the necessity we hold—all of us—to receive all of ourselves, to come to know who we are in ourselves. To these women, too, I am most grateful. Women friends have been of great help in deepening my insight and enlarging my appreciation for how much women may give each other. My enthusiastic thanks go to Staley Hitchcock for his expert deciphering of my manuscripts, his excellent typing, and his unfailing courtesy and helpfulness to me. The staff at Westminster also deserve warm thanks. Lastly my boundless thanks to my husband, Barry, who has been in so many ways my great receiver.

ANN BELFORD ULANOV

Union Theological Seminary
New York, New York

Receiving Woman

1
Receiving Woman

The title *Receiving Woman* asserts three meanings: a woman who receives herself, a woman who receives what is other than herself, and a woman who is received by others. A modern woman with a strong sense of her identity as a woman is not content with her own awareness of herself. She wants to receive others, men and women alike, in their individuality and to be received by them in her concrete identity as a woman who knows what it means to be a woman. She wants to be known as an individual and not simply a reflection of gender or anatomy. She refuses to reduce herself or others to parts of themselves, or to types or abstractions, robbed of personal life.

1. RECEIVING HERSELF

A receiving woman rejects the partial version of herself in the old stereotypes of the female, such as the hausfrau or helpmate; also the new stereotypes—feminist, political activist, career person, and nothing else. A woman receiving all of herself carries within her the conviction that you do not come to yourself either by subtraction or by abstraction. To call feminine only those qualities of compassion and nurture traditionally associated with women omits essential pieces of a woman's reality—power, intellect, aggression. To take

15

away from a woman her vaunted softness and interiority, leaving only capacities for anger and a warrior-like boldness, equally distorts her reality, abstracting and concentrating on one kind of element to define a much larger whole. A receiving woman would really receive all of herself, and not settle for less.

The hard-line male chauvinist would subtract from woman her physical power, her intellect, her ambition, her capacity for free assertion. There is a fear of these elements of her being. But even more, and more unconsciously, there is fear of the "masculine elements" of personality that exist alongside a woman's most womanly qualities—her involvement with the origins of being through her roles as child bearer and nurturer. How could she possibly have access to both modalities of being: independent assertion in the world and creation of culture on the one hand, and intimate involvement with the dependent origins of human life on the other? The result is nothing less than fear of the female, repressed but firmly present in quantities of people, women as well as men. They try to manage their fear by controlling woman's place in the world. For them, women must be confined to set roles in home and nursery, and excluded from full legal, economic, or social equality. Such people brand those of us who fight for full equality for women as disordered in our own femininity. For them the problem is clearly ours, not theirs, and it is essentially psychological. Their attitudes have long been translated into every kind of discrimination against women, reducing reality in half, insisting on a one-sided, one-dimensional view of sex: females are only female, men are only male. Thus both sexes are in effect discriminated against, diminished in rigorously prescribed sexual roles.

Hard-line feminists abstract woman from her own particular life at the dependent, vulnerable core of human being. They attack any image of the female that significantly differs from the male or from the symbolism that clusters around the masculine mode of being. They reject what they derisively call the "special nature" of women, even labeling their own sisters "soft" feminists as opposed to their preferred "hard" feminism. Soft feminism recognizes differences between the sexes and fights for equal standing for the female in society. Hard feminism repudiates any distinguishing of qualities of woman as a mere perpetuation of stereotyped sexual roles. The unconscious assumption is that sexual differences must translate into sexual discrimination against women. Those who hold this view blame woman's suffering exclusively on the political injustice systemic to society. Any psychological component in the fear of the female and what she represents is ignored as if inquiry into such factors might reveal more than their egos could take.

Stereotypes, old or new, place woman in a passive position, defined by abstract prescriptions, to which she must conform or risk attack by the stereotyping group. Many women are beginning to understand that they can no more be determined in their inmost selves by the old benevolent patriarchy than by the new malevolent sexism. New stereotypes are no less coercive than old ones. No great distance exists between "All real women marry and bear children" and "All real women know that men are sexists and rapists at heart." These opposing views are simply two sides of the same coin. In both, woman is a passive victim, determined by forces outside herself that she may resist, but is all but helpless to change. Some feminists take up this position of woman as victim so vigorously that their conviction of woman's capacity for self-determination is belied. It may reflect in displaced form their own psychological struggle with forces within themselves. In this view woman is left angry, wailing even, but stuck where she is, using up all her energies to get free from powers larger than herself.

Stereotypes seduce us into defining persons according to generalized categories. A woman bent on receiving all of herself knows well that women do not exist in the abstract. There is no one type of woman, no general woman; there are only particular women, differing each from the other. She does not label herself as one more item mass-produced on an assembly line of culture. She knows herself as a specific person living in a particular time, formed by a tradition yet with every possibility to shape her own personal style of being. In reality she is alive to and related with her world.

She knows in herself, even if not yet altogether clearly, that the female has her own way of being and cannot be defined from a male or pseudo-male point of view. Even Freud, who first insisted that a little girl's Electra complex was the converse of the little boy's Oedipal struggle, finally asserted his puzzlement about women's nature and "what they really want."[1] For the answer, he advised, we must go to women themselves and to the poets. Thus Freud, so often vilified by modern-day feminists as the great denigrator of woman, intuitively sensed the radical difference of the female self from the male. Equally important, he sensed that the way to understand woman must come from woman herself, and from the poetic image, which stands in sharp contrast to scientific investigation. Jung made the illuminating discovery that a man tends to experience the deep aspects of the unconscious as presented to him in the feminine images of the anima archetype, which he feels as something like his own soul. On this basis Jung tried to say that feminine psychology is the obverse of the masculine, and that a woman experiences her unconscious as a masculine spirit—the animus. This contention has not held up, as I tried to show in my book *The Feminine* and in the book I wrote with my husband, *Religion and the Unconscious*.[2] A woman finds her soul-link in distinctly feminine terms. The feminine cannot be grasped as simply the converse, obverse, or reverse of masculine psychology.

Receiving all of herself, a woman can shun both ancient and modern stereotypes. She can exercise her own independent judgment and focus on the concrete persons that women were and are.

In her sense of solidarity with all women, old and new, she can find support for her own efforts to receive all of herself in the present.

Women were not discovered in the 1960's, or even the earlier part of this century. Women were around and serious notice was taken of them centuries and even millennia ago. We need to pay attention to history, where we find examples that cut across stereotypes. In dialogue with older cultures we find what we thought was our own original, modern point of view. In religious and cultural traditions we find our many faces reflected in the faces of men and women of the past. Many writers crafted their understanding of being itself in woman's image.[3] Ariosto in the *Orlando Furioso* described women in battle, warriors heroically fighting for their beliefs, but no less female for doing so. Beatrice and Isabella D'Este in Ferrara were the engaging equals, at the very least, of the men at their court, not preaching what women ought to do, but demonstrating what in fact they did. Many other women of the Italian Renaissance also conveyed the singular truth about the personal core of any human being: I belong to no one but myself; who wants me must do battle with me. Theirs was hardly a view of woman as a contingent being, waiting for direction from the man in her life to define herself. This sixteenth-century notion of being is recast in twentieth-century speculation about the nature of the human psyche. D. W. Winnicott, noted for his investigations into the origins of human identity in the earliest infant-parent relationship, writes of this same inviolable center of life: "In terms of emotional acceptance the self, at its core, is always personal, isolated and unaffected by experience."[4] Examining what she found unsatisfactory in a sexual relationship, a contemporary woman said of herself in relation to her partner: "He must win me; I am not given casually or cheaply."[5]

A woman receiving all of herself looks to a culture out of which she was born and particularly to the cultural past of all women.

By inspecting the past through the work of women artists we find intimations of being human which we all need, which we all desire, which are there for us to find. In finding them, we find a space in which we are reflected back to ourselves in our discovery of being.

Helen Frankenthaler shows essential configurations of being in her giant abstractions of female anatomy. Anna Ahkmatova knew her own authority as a poet; her "unveiled" muse, unmistakably female, admits with becoming humor to being Dante's inspiration too—in the writing of his Hell (the *Inferno*). Nadezhda Mandelstam sums up the helpless vulnerability we all feel in her depiction of her own terror as she waits in line day after day outside a prison for some small word of her poet-husband's fate. She symbolizes the human capacity to take joy in what remains despite massive deprivation, to focus on the good in the midst of evil, in describing her pleasure in giving the one egg she had had for weeks to a beloved guest in her home. She conveys the horror and suffering of being treated as a nonperson in her description of the cheerless, dusty, treeless landscape that greeted her and her husband in the first of their many places of exile. Zenaida Hippius, poet and storyteller and meditative mind, describes sin as petty thinking, not self-love but being-in-love-with-self. She describes it as a life without either damnation or prayer, previewing the highly technical investigations of narcissism by such psychoanalysts as Otto Kernberg and Heinz Kohut in the 1970's. Gertrud von Le Fort, the German writer of woman's interior passions in love and in faith, gives the lie to the masochism attributed to the female by walking directly into its tangled neurotic threads and uncovering there the mystery of surrender to Christ. Even in our weaknesses and our illnesses we may win through to acts of nobility and courage. Thus Blanche de la Force, in Von Le Fort's *The Song at the Scaffold*, a woman who cannot conquer her neurotic fears, finally sees those very fears as her offering to Christ. Through them she participates in his presence, not in the joy of his love or the triumph of his resurrection, but in his agony at Gethsemane. This early-twentieth-century writer anticipates the essential question raised by depth psychology in the later part of the century: What is the difference between health and life, between being functional and being alive and caught up in a life of value?

Mrs. Gaskell's nineteenth-century heroines show us the rigors of introspection that put every feeling and perception into that inner order which produces a woman of great inward authority, one who can change the world around her through her impact on persons who come into contact with her. Mrs. Gaskell bridges the dichotomy between the private and public realms of life that so bedevil our times. Her novels are among the first of what is sometimes called a sociological genre, taking up issues of class and economy. The clashes of factory workers and masters in her books yield resolution only through persons achieving insight into the common humanity they share.[6] Her heroines are quite different from those superficial talkers who "lashed themselves up into an enthusiasm about high subjects in company, and never thought about them when they were alone; they squandered their capabilities of appreciation into a mere flow of appropriate words."[7]

Mrs. Gaskell reminds women today that each of us in our own identities does not have to do it all and indeed cannot do it all. Her heroines achieve a wide and deep capacity to trust the life in them to take its proper shape, to flow through them and to provide what they must have. They trust other people to see them as they are. They need not become everything in themselves nor explain everything nor attempt the omnipotent feats that so often tempt women in our time—to put into words truths that come only in nondiscursive forms. These heroines trust life to come into being. They do not expect themselves to be and do and tell everything. They recognize and accept the veiled truth whose unveiling reveals more hidden truths. They respect the pauses as part of a human continuity. They let go of their humanness and allow the divine to come in. They let being be, without taking their own efforts to be the crux of whatever happens. They trust in the power of their presence, of their inward being, to be recognized and received by others. This letting-be permits bold, sustained action when particular personal effort is really called for. Removed from the omnipotent center of the world, these heroines take up their specific concrete responsibility in the world all the more vigorously.

2. BEING RECEIVED

We live now in a historical era of unparalleled opportunities for fundamental changes of consciousness. There are accessible to us in increasingly articulated form the images, concepts, and symbols of the feminine modality of being. These can be added to—not subtracted from or substituted for—the masculine, to give us our understanding of what it is to be human. We have begun to be liberated from the mutually exclusive dualisms of spirit and flesh, heaven and earth, active and passive, penetration and reception, that traditionally have been symbolized in the images of masculine and feminine and set against each other as polarized opposites. For a time these original distinctions helped us articulate the fundamental dynamics of our experience. Over the years they have become increasingly rigid and sapped of their symbolic power as they have been applied more and more as prescriptions for the identities of actual men and women. In recent decades these divisive categories have lost some of their hold on us. Women's challenges liberated all of us to some extent from their prescriptive tyranny, but we have not yet integrated the modalities of being human that they symbolize, not yet secured them for conscious disposal.

Women who would receive all of themselves and who insist on being received by others as all of themselves, lead the way at the moment in shaping what could become a radically new consciousness. A woman wanting to receive all of herself faces the feminine as it is, in its own right, accepting the shaping influences of her female biology, of the history of women, of the distinct cluster of imagery and affect traditionally symbolized as the feminine. Shunning those reductions that equate recognition of the feminine to passive subscription to double standards, and shunning the notion that if one denies the distinct existence of female persons as female, somehow all problems will disappear, she embarks on a third course. She actively inquires what it might mean in a variety of ways to approach things from a distinctly feminine point of view. Hers is neither the univocal one-sex view, nor the equivocal no-difference-between-the-sexes view. Her view reaches toward a larger totality and a concomitant enlargement of consciousness, to what might properly be called a religious view. It includes a strong emphasis on women shaping their own styles of personal identity in response to their cultural heritage, the influence of their bodies, and the symbols long associated with the feminine. It centers on an openness to the guiding impulses of spirit that herald a new vision of woman as containing within herself a masculine side as man has a feminine side. It is a spirit particularly manifest in the Christian faith, where God called out woman to bring the Divine into the world in the flesh, as a human person in whom we can find our own persons.

The receiving woman, then, begins with the feminine and with the female's psychology. Each woman is seen in her own right, guided by her own intrinsic psychological and spiritual qualities. Women can and do show their own distinct ways of being human, and in the history of symbols the feminine does offer a cluster of images with a vast number of associated emotional and behavioral patterns that gather specific equipment and endowments as modes of human reality. These must now be explored. What does this mean in practical terms?

In Scripture studies, for example, it means that we approach the texts from a perspective that shows us the feminine as present even if it is a presence marked by absence. What was so fearful about the feminine mode of being that was transferred to females that they were so long excluded from leading places in society? In the Old Testament, we must not only focus on the repudiation of the feminine in the forbidding of the worship of mother goddesses that competed with loyalty to Yahweh, but we must also investigate the new vision of the feminine and of the place of women in Yahwist faith.[8] Was some new intimation of the interweaving of masculine and feminine modalities of being human moving toward the construction of a new human identity? Do we find this vision reached for again in the modern Jewish woman's embrace of the ancient tradition of *mikvah,* the ritual cleansing after each menstrual period?[9] What are we to make of such participants' claims that they recover an innate rhythm of the female body that promotes a fluctuating curve of sexual relations—that sustains a greater sexual excitement within the ordinary humdrum patterns of daily life? Further, these women say they experience an intrinsic connection between the ebbs and flows of their menstrual tides and their religious devotions.

In the New Testament, Jesus approaches women in a radical way—seeing them as capable of receiving the first announcements of revolutionary theological declarations. Martha, so often maligned as the overactive housekeeper, is the first person to hear from Jesus that he is the resurrection and the life. The promiscuous and alien Samaritan woman hears from Jesus that he brings the living water of the Spirit and that when we have drunk from it we cannot die. Mary, Jesus' mother, hears from her Son's lips that even the inextricable bonds of maternal instinct are severed by the Word of God that claims prior allegiance. These statements smash the conventional definitions of the woman's role both in those times and in our own. Jesus did not treat these women either with patronizing coddling or with condescending superiority. He met them head on and spoke to their singular beings wrapped in their own self-definitions and in their cultural roles. He called them out to be all of themselves in relation to the God he proclaimed. A vast new territory of scriptural study waits to be developed, focusing upon the feminine modality of being human that is present in our Judeo-Christian tradition.

Similarly in economics, while the destructive prejudice against working women is exposed, new attempts must be instigated to create patterns and possibilities of employment for women that heretofore have not existed. The many women in their middle years, gifted with intelligence, motivation, and energy, are a great resource. They need to be challenged and directed to business, to professional careers, service agencies, and political causes, not just for their sakes, but for all of us and our society. Unused energies clog the social atmosphere with resentment. We need these women and what they have to offer; we need new styles of jobs, new conceptions of work hours, and new mixtures of work and play instead of increased pressure to get more money and more leisure time for which we are largely unprepared. A vicious cycle of pressure to get and pressure to spend, without innate satisfaction either in work or play, sets up a social time bomb of accumulated frustration and unhappiness. Its explosion comes in mental breakdowns and homicidal, suicidal, and political violence.

Religious experience teaches us to look to the feminine directly. Through what have been thought of as the "curses" of menstruation and childbearing, women find themselves equipped with insight into a central element of religion.[10] These somatic female rhythms echo a rhythm of spirit hard to achieve and yet so necessary to religious life—giving consent of will to God's direction.

Literal birth-giving is paradigmatic for all kinds of metaphorical birth-giving in the creative arts, in intense love, and in religious experience. We learn in all of these to yield to a will that moves in us but is not our own, that does not snuff out our own will, but moves ours strongly into accord with its own. Such an experience marks us forever. We know in it simultaneous mixtures of self and other, flesh and spirit, strong emotion and intellectual reflection. Women realize this will at an instinctual level. Monthly cramps that will not be subdued by drugs dictate that we withdraw, go to bed, retire into ourselves, whether we want to or not. Our schedules are rearranged in response to the voice of our bodies. Similarly, in childbirth, with all our modern medical techniques, we wait on the hidden moment of conception, never sure it will occur. We wait for the body to announce the coming birth. Even with the techniques of induced labor, we wait until the body signals the beginning of the birth process. We wait to receive. We wait to assist the movement of the child into life with our own strenuous efforts. Alert to promptings beyond our control, we stand ready to consent. A woman learns this central pull on her at the level of instinct, through the guidance of her own body, as if she had, as a fairy-tale character has, a wise animal like a horse to take her to the treasure. Our bodies can give us this horse sense.

To know she possesses personal access, in her own body, to this experience of cooperation with a life force beyond her control gives a woman a special spiritual potential. The experience of being a woman, in touch with a larger reality that religion speaks of, she views not as nullifying her personal identity but as enlarging it. Many women active in the women's movement who have lost their faith glimpse its beginnings again in their experience with this larger reality. For them the women's movement carries the numinous aura of a larger presence that affirms their own ways of being female.

Women bound on receiving all of themselves approach everything differently, from personal relationships to disciplines of study and their professional lives. They experiment with new ways of bringing together, combining, recombining, synthesizing, separating, and integrating the masculine and feminine elements of themselves. They act as trailblazers for the rest of us in enlarging consciousness beyond sexual roles to a new sensibility to the contrasexual dimensions of persons. They give examples in the everyday details of life of how to do the original thing, how consciously to create new syntheses of masculine and feminine, how not to regress to their split forms—either the old one of being just female, mother and wife, or the new one of a female indistinguishable from a male. They accept those differences between male and female and the modes of being symbolized as masculine and feminine as belonging in many different ways to members of both sexes. In receiving those differences they find a basis for similarity among all of us, men and women alike, that changes and enlarges our shared life, public and private.

These women receive the male and female elements of being and work them into an effective and personal identity, which is the opposite of passive conformity to prescribed roles. They struggle to bring these elements together, no longer settling for family at the sacrifice of career, or for a job at the cost of a relationship. They find different and entirely personal ways to bring these aspects of life together so that each benefits the other. That is new.

3. RECEIVING OTHERS

What is also strikingly new about these receiving women is that they put forth no collective model, no "correct" way of how a woman should act. Instead, they show us many routes. Different women have different ways of combining or recombining, adding to or subtracting masculine elements from their feminine being. For example, a forty-eight-year-old woman with her children all but grown begins her work on a Ph.D., laying the groundwork for a distinguished career in one of the helping fields. A woman of twenty-one marries during her last year in college. She and her husband go to graduate school together, seeking their careers while they build their home together. She interweaves her commitment to women's liberation with her love for her husband. Another woman in her thirties, having begun her career, takes time out to bear a child and time out to find the motivating center of her work that can only benefit from her increased capacity to nurture. Another married woman in her late twenties begins her career while holding in abeyance the possibility of having her first child within the next few years. Juggling career and family, she acknowledges the elements of chance, contingency, surprise as factors in the decision. Another woman, married and divorced in her mid-twenties, takes the pain of a ruptured relationship to galvanize her latent courage to act on a long-hidden ambition to pursue a career of her own. She has had to shed a shell of conformity to a housewifely image in order to crack open what she experiences in her work as her true center. A woman in her thirties pursues a career, open to relationship but not at all sure marriage or motherhood is for her. A woman in her fifties leaves her marriage of many years because she knows it to have been a pretense that damaged both parties and their children. She is not at all certain who she is or where she belongs. By seizing the outer truth she hopes to find her way to the inner one. Though criticized by her ex-husband as selfish in her action of divorce, she believes she gives a gift to him and to their children: an example, even if confused and groping, of trying to live out who one truly is. She finds this less painful and more life-giving than persisting in a false identity. Still another woman in her fifties, dedicated to her husband and children, sees herself at a point in life where she can mix all she has been as a wife and mother with the development of her talent as an artist.

These are examples of specific women who put together tradition and originality, the problems and possibilities of being human, feminine and masculine elements of being. Such qualities become concrete in their individual temperaments, tempos, problems, and relationships to all that is other in their lives—to specific pasts, specific biological realities, specific symbols of the feminine. They introduce and underscore particularity as essential to being human. They make us see that we do our best work not by leveling down to a category, but by including in our lives all the personal variables. These efforts by individual women offer us models for collective patterns of employment, for humanizing work through an assertion of sexual differences, for a realistic exchange between the private and public dimensions of life without sacrificing either.

It is a great sin to tell such pioneering, self-assertive, model-making women that theirs is a "selfish endeavor," that they are involved in some "bourgeois illusion," that they are retreating into a "privatistic indulgence" while neglecting the world's injustices. Such an attack attempts to draw them away from their personal life into abstractions, from the concrete elements of their own being into empty generality; steering them away from an active and receptive consciousness into what must be for them a senseless struggle. This attack sabotages efforts to create out of parts of life a living, personal whole, both as individuals and as members of communities; as loving persons receptive to other persons. It altogether misses the fact that they are persons firm enough in their own identities to receive otherness in all its forms—other cultures, other ways of looking at the same tasks, other ways to conceive meaning in life, above all the otherness of truth. Only a woman receiving her own identity can be open to otherness with all its religious implications. These women attempt the new and know it as a fragile undertaking. Their effort is much more difficult than denouncing the failures of tradition. Their course of life is much more subject to doubt than that of the accusers of others. They seek new channels of personal life, of wider consciousness to include in a female fullness of personal identity what heretofore has been split up between the sexes.

Into this vigorous yet delicate task comes a woman's capacity to receive others as concrete persons. With a history of second-class citizenship, a symbolism of neglect, and massive projections cast on her as a female, a woman who comes to terms with all of herself is particularly sensitive to the left-out, neglected, or scorned parts of other persons. Concrete and personal in her own reality, she is aware of the violence done by the abstract categorization of others. She can receive the particularity of the other. She knows the value of personal experience. Her capacity to combine the actual and the theoretical, the concrete and the general, suggests new ways of thinking about being, both theologically and in the daily life of faith. Her reception of others brings with it a confidence in full reciprocity, that others will receive her also.

Receiving woman's reception of herself and her reception by others inaugurates a new understanding of what it means to be human. Like Eve initiating knowledge of good and evil, and like Mary initiating a reconciliation of the human and the Divine, she shows special insight into the hiddenness of God's revelation. God's presence, she shows us, emerges in concrete situations and particular lives, not in abstract generalization or rhetorical labels in which persons do not really exist at all. The pattern of discovery is of a God who remains veiled even when unveiled, a being who loses no mystery by becoming accessible. Probing being in its concreteness takes us further and further into the presence of mystery, a presence that does not lend itself to verbal statement but only summons us to receive it in concrete experience.

The following chapters elaborate these themes. Chapter 2 explores the detours of discrimination against women, those that reduce her to the old stereotypes of wife and mother or their surrogates, those that deny there is anything special or particular about feminine existence in the stereotyping of the new hard-line feminists. Either women are told to stay in their place, or they are told to cease thinking of themselves as women altogether, for they are no different from men. The third detour, into androgyny, again obliterates the distinct existence of the female as female and the symbols of the feminine. All these detours lead to dead ends, because the sexual differentiation of men and women is neither the problem facing women today nor the root of discrimination against us. The problem springs from another source: failure to understand what the differentiation really means. The issue is not the distinct feminine modality of being but how we respond to it.

Chapter 3 will relocate the source of the issue in our fear of receiving woman and the mode of being that the feminine symbolizes. Instead of receiving that feminine mode of being, we project it out of ourselves into stereotypes, which we apply to women in unconscious efforts to gain some measure of control over what we fear. The problem lies in the processes of projection, and the solution lies in receiving instead of disowning these aspects of being. The mechanism of projection will be examined along with the radical impact on consciousness when we withdraw such projections and assimilate them to our own self-images.

Chapter 4 takes up the question of what these feminine elements of being really are and why we should see them as feminine, and not just human. I will argue that our fear of them forms the root of hatred against the female. We seek to control many of our fears by projecting these elements of being onto women and confining them to a subordinate position in society. We either try to stereotype the female or repress awareness of her distinct reality. A double displacement occurs, one of content and one of attitude. There follows a displacement of what the feminine symbolizes onto concrete females, and a displacement of fear onto hatred of those elements of being. These displacements have a disastrous effect on our social and political life. Thus, withdrawing projections brings major consequences for society.

Chapter 5 relates the insight derived from the female experience of conception, pregnancy, and birth to the nascent stages of the spiritual life. The growth of such experience is essential if we expect to reverse the double displacement and come to receive instead of fear and hate those core aspects of human being.

Chapter 6 investigates what it means concretely for a woman to integrate what Jung calls the animus, the masculine side of herself. The common pitfall in that undertaking—the split-animus state—and the peculiar authority that attends its success will be discussed. If a receiving woman rejects propaganda urging her to shed the feminine elements of her being in order to achieve an exclusively virile ego, she just as forcefully repels efforts to reduce and confine her to traditional female roles. The images of the women's movement—women on the move, women liberated, women on the march, women stepping out—capture the energy and dedication of women to claim all of themselves. The receiving woman wants to appropriate for her ego's use all those undeveloped, unconscious capacities to produce and to do which the animus mediates to her awareness and which she or society may think of as masculine. She is not content with less than all of herself.

Chapter 7 concludes the book with an exploration of the distinct potentialities that a receiving woman brings into the world and ministers to others with particular grace in the areas of pain, human rejection, acknowledgment of evil, and perception of the hiddenness of God's revelation.

2
Detours to Dead Ends

Regardless of what wing of the feminist movement we favor, or if we favor none at all, most of us can agree that sexual stereotyping is dehumanizing. The construction of hard-and-fast roles for all who want to become "real men" and "real women" not only stunts the lives of particular persons but often comes close to murder in the constrictions those roles demand. Persons are measured against sex roles, judged and inevitably found wanting, because actual persons, with their idiosyncratic variations on human themes, can never fulfill an abstract role with its various generalities. In fact, such role demands become weapons of attack against persons fighting to outlaw sexual discrimination. How often one hears, "Only a woman disturbed in her own femininity would want to hold a job that has traditionally belonged to men." Or, "Only men insecure in their masculinity, under the thumb of mother or wife, would knuckle under to the demand for equal pay and promotion for females." Worse still is the long history of prejudice against women who have been treated across the world as the property of males, identified with childbearing, excluded from positions of leadership, not only hedged around by massive expectations to carry the nurturant functions of life but considered disposable if the investment made in them proved unsatisfactory.

Reification of sexual difference into prescribed social places, transmitted through stereotyped sex roles, acts as a means of sometimes flagrant, sometimes subtle injustice against women. Examples are countless.

THE FIRST DETOUR

We must reject outright the first option offered as a means of dealing with sexual difference through prescriptive stereotypes: that of assigning prepackaged psychological characteristics, social roles, and legal definitions exclusively to one sex or the other. This path is precisely the one most people now recognize as a detour, leading far away from a just and humane human community. Thanks in large measure to the women's movement, our collective consciousness of either subtle or gross discrimination against women is now greatly increased and the defense of this position is all but untenable. We recognize that women are simply not received as all of themselves in this way, but rather are reduced to parts of themselves, treated as dispensers of the commodities of mother love, home care, sexual satisfaction, and moral values. Obviously, we cannot afford to lose what women have to offer in these central areas. But neither can we restrict the values, skills, and inclinations involved to the female province alone.

First, we must ask how the sexual stereotypes are formed. How did the distinctions perceived between men and women and elaborated upon in the powerful symbols of masculine and feminine become so sapped of power, so flattened of levels of meaning, that they degenerated into destructive labels, pasted onto people out of fear and hatred?

Stereotypes originate in a step-by-step process. Perception of sexual difference is frozen into hard-and-fast definitions, and then into prescriptive sex roles. The existence in society of reified, prescriptive sexual stereotyping presupposes an antecedent radical splitting up of that central and early perception of otherness which is inherent in sexual polarity. This radical splitting arises out of fear of the female and what the feminine symbolizes in the human condition, a fear usually ignored as attention is riveted instead on sexual polarity as the cause of discrimination against women.[1]

Behind sexual discrimination and the abusive application of sexual stereotypes lies the psychological repression of sexual polarity. The masculine and feminine poles act as central symbols in describing all of life's polarities. They give images and imaginative elaboration to the human experience of difference and otherness, both presupposing and building a culture of images that express human reality. They move in a symbolic universe describing generalized human experience, not simply this man or that woman. When sexual labels turn up, this world of symbolic images has been radically truncated, flattened out, and reduced almost beyond recognition. The original dynamic tension of paired opposites is violently split apart into a polarized dualism, pitting sex against sex in a competitive struggle for supremacy. Difference is then experienced as hostile to identity and canceling it, rather than as enlivening and encouraging the expression of all of one's nature.

· This psychological breaking down of dynamic pairs of opposite images and energies distorts human experience and makes possible an acting out of this inward splitting in systems of social oppression. For example, the symbols of the feminine as meek, mild, and gentle, when severed from their obvious opposite signs, those that are excited, heroic, or forceful, undergo such distortion that the feminine comes to be equated with only one extreme. Thus a woman's qualities become ripe for reification and application as stereotypes. Woman now is defined as weak and trembling like a frightened rabbit. What a loss for both sexes! Rarely in liturgical worship do we celebrate Mary as a figure of fierce aggressive capacities who singly held herself open to God's presence, without support of reason or conventions of her culture. Only another female, Elizabeth, who found herself in an almost equally anomalous position, gave Mary company.

At a primary symbolic level all strong human tendencies undergo distortion without the modifying influence of their opposites. Meekness, mildness, and gentleness degenerate into timidity, cloying dependency, spineless softness. Excitedness, forcefulness, and heroism are exacerbated into agitated harshness, pushiness, noisy self-aggrandizement. On social levels, this psychological splitting is played out in prescribing—positively demanding—a meek role for the female, destined to be "protected" at home, while the heroic role is reserved for the male, who lives out there in the "real world." The woman confined to meekness with insufficient scope for her own forcefulness falls victim to this unlived side of herself. Her forcefulness finds indirect outlets in strategies planned to promote her husband's career or in covert directing of her children's lives. She is then accused of not being a "real woman" because of her aggressive intrusions into others' lives. No wonder women consume themselves in resentment! What other outlet is left for them?

Perhaps the worst effect of stereotyping is the false carving up of the world into private and public domains that accompanies it. With the female assigned to be keeper of a gentleness that finds no effective place in a so-called man's world, unmodified harshness and untempered heroics reign as the necessary adjunct of the pursuit of political and economic success. In this construction of sexual worlds, the values associated with women are those considered impractical, not functional in the world of politics and economics. The values of power and of high accomplishment involved with getting ahead in the world are assumed not to go with the softer feminine sensibilities. The result is a situation of great peril for all of us. The present violent divisions in our world, on almost every level, bear terrible testimony to this fact.

The reversal of these roles does not offer much comfort either. With the female in a superior position, the male is reduced to second-class roles, a merely tangential sexuality. Women can band together to exclude men. They can insist on special spaces to be assigned to them alone, lobby for their own exclusive professional positions and for courses of study devoted only to them. In many ways such demands are understandable, and it is hard not to be sympathetic toward them. The female and the symbolism of the feminine have so long been neglected and abused that in recovering them to full consciousness women need to support one another. A sense of a common base and a place of their own for sharing permits them to be altogether themselves and thus to receive themselves as who and what they are. Too often, however, the task of self-discovery stops at mere form reversal, women defining themselves negatively at the expense of men. Then the stereotyping failures and reductions begin all over again. Women pride themselves on their patent superiority. Men are treated with prejudice, cast in stereotyped roles, and viewed with a familiar scorn that reflects all the *a priori* assumptions from which women have suffered.

The central question arises: Must sexual polarity always, inevitably degenerate into violent polarization? Must we always fall into destructive battles for supremacy? Do images of sexual polarity ineluctably lead to reified sexual stereotypes that promote social discrimination? Must our patterns always be those of dominance or submission, superiority or inferiority? Or is there an alternative path, where perception of sexual difference can promote psychological differentiation, where images of sexual polarity can inspire reciprocity and mutuality? Do we not have in our time an opportunity for a different line of development, where sexual polarity confronts us with the possibility of widening and deepening consciousness to hold both modalities of being human in simultaneous awareness?

THE SECOND DETOUR

If sexual polarity inevitably turns into polarization of the sexes, if perception of sexual difference necessarily produces discrimination against women—or men—we embark on a second detour by which sexual difference can be dealt with and the abuse of women combatted. This is the attempt to annihilate the image of sexual polarity altogether. It is a strong course of action indeed. It starts with a hatred of every image of sexual distinction.

Those passionately opposed to the social injustice of a sexism that fosters all kinds of superiority-inferiority dualism attack the problem of discrimination against women with a corrosive contempt for sexual polarity. Their attack focuses both on concrete sexual differences and on images that symbolize the masculine and feminine as fundamental expressions of the modalities of the human.

Many women of my generation who have been, as I have, the only woman in a class of men, the only woman in a training program, the first woman in a particular job, are in sympathy with this attack. The isolation caused by a great wall of negative and positive expectations built around you by your colleagues proves painful indeed. You are not seen as a particular person, but rather as the carrier of an abstract category called "woman," meaning differently accented assumptions for each of your colleagues! It often seems as if nothing can break down this wall. Rather, you sense that you are always being compared to a set of flatly assumed characteristics, and hence you are always encumbered by a list of psychic measurements as prescriptive as the old-fashioned set of the right numbers for the ideal female figure. Great anger arises from the pain of being seen this way—or rather not being seen. Your presence has, in effect, been nullified.

This pain that so quickly converts to anger can lead women to a hatred of all images of sexual polarity. If no notion of sexual differences existed, either of the concrete or the symbolic, so the reasoning goes, then no reification of those differences into constricting stereotypes could occur. Annihilate those images of sexual polarity, and prejudice against women will go. What often follows is fantasies of social violence. A curious alliance between feminism and radical politics emerges and a political identity replaces sexual identity.

Women under these pressures want to attack the whole society that permits sexual discrimination. They see sexual polarity as the root of all the pernicious dualisms in modern society. The polarization of the sexes is the inevitable result of recognizing sexual differences. The complementary, dynamic, and reciprocal relation between the sexes depicted in the image of sexual polarity cannot stand. It must split apart into a hostile dualism of men against women or vice versa.

The argument goes on: We must rid ourselves of the notion of sexual polarity altogether and thus expunge the sadism of such polarizations as rich and poor, East and West, left and right. Destroy all images of polarity by obliterating the central one of sexuality. Anything less will only help preserve the covering on our corrupt social system and make remedies for our sick society harder and harder to prescribe, for we will not be able to see the illnesses beneath the sexual disguises. Violent rhetoric comes with simplistic thinking. The cure is to smash the society that supports the image and the image that breeds the rotten society. What begins as an anguished cry for inclusion of the specific presence of women ends in a global attack on all of society and rejects the very existence of widely disparate persons.

Hatred of the image of sexual polarity, like most hatreds, leads to a dead end. Sexuality gives us a primary and universal experience of difference. It acts as a paradigm for most of life's tensions, contrasts, and oppositions. The masculine-feminine polarity turns up in psychic material and in the world's mythologies and religions as a principal symbol for both the interconnectedness and the divisive competition between basic pairs of opposites. In it are expressed the psychological processes of conscious and unconscious, affiliation and negation. It reflects such mythological realms as heaven and earth, light and darkness, sun and moon, logos and eros.

Every effort to annihilate the images of sexual polarity amounts to little more than repressing them into the unconscious. There, dissociated from the civilizing influence of the ego, the image regresses to more primitive states and contaminates whatever else remains unconscious. Repressing sexual polarity amounts to denying the evidence of our senses, of body differences, and of the reception of the psychological significance of those differences. To repress this knowledge requires huge expenditures of energy that builds up enormous tension in the unconscious. This sets the stage for the inevitable return of the repressed content by devious routes, usually in heightened agitation about almost all other polarities, as if conscripting them to play the central symbolic role that sexual symbolism so long enjoyed.

We see evidence for this interpretation in the displacement of sexual polarization onto political polarizations, best summed up by the dualism of oppressor and oppressed. The feminists who reject images of sexual polarity show a particular fondness for this set of stereotypes. Just as hatred of sexual imagery leads to all-out political attacks on society as we know it in the West, so the prescriptive sexual stereotypes are transmogrified into rigidly prescriptive roles for political activists, insisting on an "us-them" mentality. The sequence is clear: sexual polarity is perceived as a hostile polarization of the sexes; therefore the imagery of sexual polarity is repressed in hopes of cutting off injustice at its root. But this central paradigm of human behavior reemerges in its displaced forms in political polarities that quickly undergo the same inner distortion into reified stereotypes of polarized opposites. Political polarity changes into an anguished politicization with all its attendant abuses. Holders of this view fall under the same old unconscious assumption: "we" are right and "they" are wrong; hence "they" deserve every violence because "they" do not conform to our standards. Flight into abstractions occurs just as in the worst abuses of sexual stereotyping where an immutable reified content of "female" or "feminine" hangs like a moon in the sky. The content is different but the process remains the same. Political polarization encourages the timeworn utopian fantasy that we can make ourselves and our world perfect if people will only do what we say. We point to lofty abstractions and global solutions, all distant from the immediate concrete facts and problems that demand our attention. We see our cause stretching to the far horizon, ourselves conscripted into an unending fight for principles—unending because they are comfortably abstract and hypothetical, without the awkwardness and untidiness of the concrete and immediate.

The same labeling with facile slogans occurs as in the worst abuses of sexual stereotyping, the same bullying tactics and vilification of sexual identities. The "real woman" now must subscribe to a code of politicization, a code of dress, a code of behavior, that if deviated from brings down on her head the kind of ostracism suffered by the early suffragettes who deviated from children-church-kitchen formulas.

A woman dragged under by repression of sexual polarity is bound to behave in exaggeratedly oppressive ways. She is not likely to recover her own feminine identity, or to win recognition for feminine modalities in collective consciousness. Rather, she loses big chunks of her feminine ego to the unconscious, replacing it with what Jung calls animus slogans—generalized prescriptions uttered to herself and to others, both women and men, about how things ought to be. There is no bridging connection to the woman she actually is or to the concrete reality of the other person.[2] She offers others a caricature of masculine behavior, a driven, dissociated, hell-bent, bit-in-the-teeth determination to get her own way regardless of the sacrifice of values involved.

The horrible irony of this dilemma shows forth in the ardent hard-line feminist who behaves in a flagrantly sexist manner toward other women. She seeks them out for a job, for example, not on the basis of talent or qualification, but simply on the basis of anatomy, hiring by vagina. But let that candidate for employment reveal a different view of politics or of "the movement," and the ardent feminist will drop her cold, labeling her with contempt as a "good girl" or "queen bee" or "the enemy." The myth of sisterhood collapses. Any woman not holding precisely the same views is rejected and cast out. Caught in a repression of her own concrete identity as a woman, this hard-liner cannot see any other woman's concrete reality. For her there are only broad categories and narrowly applied abstractions.

The effects on general political life of such constricting sexual politics prove equally unfortunate. Acquiring as it does a displacement of sexual energy onto its own political procedures, the procedures in turn take on a frenzied, agitated quality, full of the restless tensions of unlived sexual emotion. Like an animal in sexual season, persons caught in obsessive politicization compulsively sniff for potential issues, prowl in search of grievances, seek a suitable injustice on which to vent their undischarged energies. A "rally round the flag, boys" mentality is generated, whipping up emotions for the cause. Such emotions can quickly turn into their opposites, love and hate switching roles with frightening rapidity.

Edith Weigert's analysis of regressive group organization comes to mind.[3] Not just the group superego but each personal ego is projected onto the leader or cause being fought for. Its fate gets tangled with everyone's personal fate. Who one is rests perilously on the outcome of political struggles, on victory or defeat. One does not consciously lend ego support to the cause, based on convictions of value, or withdraw support for like reasons. Rather, one's ego is delivered over to unconscious identification with a cause. Thus even in victory the ego knows defeat, feeling itself a passive victim in the grip of forces beyond one's control. The ego forsakes autonomy and self-management to merge unconsciously with the group mind. Regression ensues to a pre-ego state of being. One is carried along in a current of generalized views and collective emotions, abstract positions that do not concern the concrete life of persons struggling to build relationship to each other.[4]

A woman caught in this undertow toward repression, regression, and group identification risks being left helpless in the tides of her own helpless anger. When she is constantly encouraged to accuse others, to condemn the system or our patriarchal culture as the cause of all injustice and her own unhappiness in particular, she is repeatedly lured away from the concrete earth of her own psychic life, from persons and issues that comprise her actual situation. Losing her ego foothold, she is set adrift in generalized frustration and anger. If her cause wins a point, her ego is often dangerously inflated. Manic elation may flood her fragilely anchored ego. If her side loses, she will be swamped by currents of rage and envy. Whichever way the outer issue goes, she remains in her inner life like a paper boat tossed about on a large sea. She has no defenses against the collective emotions around her or the instinctive reactions welling up from her own unconscious processes. She cannot deal with her own reactions because she cannot receive herself; she looks only for ways to blame the other. She rejects any urging she feels to recover conscious ego links to the various causes for her unhappiness. She makes accusations against consciousness itself as being a selfish indulgence, privatism, and elitism.

Such a woman's hostility to consciousness mirrors her rejection of herself. There can be no renewal through consciousness. Con-

sciousness and its values are illusions, mere superstructures loom-
ing over more basic political realities. She listens with an ear always
alert for the "hidden agenda." Others never say what they mean,
but always hide some threatening motive, some strategy to gain
power. Consciousness as a distinct mode of reality collapses with
her refusal to receive her own special self. Now her reality exists
only as part of a larger collective cause, and the basis for her
connection with others lies in their identifying with her cause.

POLITICIZATION: AN OPIATE FOR RAGE

Short-term benefits may appear to accrue to holders of such a
position. When we locate all injustice and unhappiness outside
ourselves, we find a place to put all our negative feelings. Politicization, in contrast to politics, acts as an opiate for anger and anxiety.
We feel justified to direct our rage at the other person, the true
villain, or toward the system which causes all the trouble in society.
Thereby we legitimize our rage, making it a force for justice. We
must show anger. We feel we have an ethical and political responsibility to vent our rage against society, even to blow it up if
necessary. Rage becomes a weapon for social change. That the
anger is excessive, overdetermined by unconscious causes, attacks
the rights of others, and foments violence, is not important.

We are relieved from exerting intellectual effort. We need not
examine opposing views, or inquire into the truth of a matter or
the complexity of an issue. Simpleminded reductions are ready at
hand. Any disagreement with our views can be automatically
labeled "sexism" or "resistance to change" or "collaboration with
oppressive regimes."

Similarly we are relieved of the hard work of introspection, for
we have found our villain outside ourselves. We need not examine
our own contributions to our anger, our labeling of those who hold
differing views, our blaming of persons in the present for those

who hurt us in the past, any injustice at all in our own actions or attitudes. These personal factors are drowned in the flood of rhetoric about collective injustice, about injustice in the large scheme of things, about "the system."

These short-term benefits come at a high cost. What is refused admission to consciousness returns by another route, from the outside. Then we take a hand in re-creating the very situations in which we have suffered rejection, misunderstanding, and attack. A woman who does not receive the person she really is—her concrete womanhood—in favor of generalized exhortations attacks her own self-respect, keeping her anger fueled. Her vigilance to detect in others any deviation from her own view of the truth injects tension into all her dealings with others. She may fall into a tightly fused identification with someone holding views like her own. But even here she fails to make room to receive herself, to claim for herself what she thinks, to understand where she is confused, or where she sees things quite differently from others. She is closed to places and positions that might change her mind. It all amounts to a refusal of herself by herself which promotes an agitated sensitivity to others' failures to receive her. She expects their rejection and engineers it unconsciously. No matter what the other person may say or do to show receptive awareness of her, she suspects a devious motive, a "hidden agenda." She meets every effort to make contact with a know-it-all attitude that finally drives others away. She cannot be reached. She is inaccessible in her fortress of preconceived opinions. Triumphant in her misery, she makes a fortissimo "I told you so! I was right all along! I knew you would reject me!"

It is not much of a triumph. She is wrecked in her relations with herself, with other women who may not agree with every one of her views, and with men. She is fixed in her role as the eternal angry victim, with no way to deal with her concrete self or situation. She has given herself over to an abstract, collectivized pro-

gram. Her life runs away from her. The days, the months, the years
go by. She does not develop but stays on a treadmill of generalized
positions, always ready to fight the next battle, having long ago lost
the war.

FAITH AND ANALYSIS

The Judeo-Christian tradition sets its tough realism against the
unreasoning hatred of polarity and the naive notion that we can
uproot it. Human existence is not perfectible; it is flawed by
splitting. Sin is splitting. The myth of the Fall can properly be read
as polarity splitting into polarization. Salvation can be read as
receiving and finding better ways to respond to human polarity.
We are saved when our consciousness enlarges and grows tough
enough to recover our disastrously polarized parts into a mutually
responsive coupling of opposites. We do not altogether end splitting this way but we do discover ways to aid the transformation
of its negative polarizations into positive polarities.

The psychoanalyst directs us back to this central insight of
Christianity: an altogether negative splitting results from stopped-
up loving, from a consciousness too small to embrace self and
other simultaneously. Harold Searles, noted for his treatment of
schizophrenia, made the startling discovery that beneath the
scorn, loathing, and hostility that characterize the relationship
between a person afflicted with schizophrenia and his or her
mother, there is "a severely repressed, most intensely anxiety-
provoking, genuine fondness for each other."[5] He notes that every
one of us, even as an infant, knows a need to give love as well as
receive it. We need to find our giving received as much as we need
to receive from others. He speculates that "lovingness is the basic
stuff of the human personality."[6] The murderous aggression so
evident in a personality invaded by schizophrenic disorder turns
out, upon examination, to be a massive defense against repressed

loving and the need to love. The preschizophrenic child will even sacrifice his or her chance for sanity, the possibility of individuality, to try to rescue a fragile, anxiety-ridden mother whose own sanity hangs in precarious balance. The child assumes the mother's illness to spare her its ravaging effects and above all not to leave her alone in her suffering. "He introjects her primarily in an effort to save her by taking her difficulties, her cross, upon himself."[7] Who would think to find this Christlike sacrifice in the depths of madness!

Similarly, the mother of a person suffering from schizophrenia unintentionally fosters this illness in her child by her very attempts to protect her child. Because of unsatisfactory relations to her own parents, a mother's capacity to love is arrested—stopped up—while still in a primitive form. Her loving exists in her as a fearsome force, undifferentiated from her aggression and her hungry impulses to devour. This force of love invades her consciousness and just as quickly retreats again because it is not securely integrated into her ego. She tries to defend her child from this sporadic and overwhelming behavior on her part by denying her love altogether. Thus while trying to save her child she drives him crazy by withholding the very love he needs to be sane.[8]

What a poignant paradigm of our human condition! We do much damage to one another when we cannot receive all that belongs to us and try instead to manufacture security for ourselves. We do much harm to others with our defenses against receiving being into ourselves. Much misery is introduced into the world with our enforced solutions for the world's ills. Many murders of soul, of emotion, of body, are committed in the name of promoting the good. We need only think of Ku Klux Klan lynchings and "liberating" revolutions of all kinds to identify with the sorrowing Christ figure shedding tears of blood over our obsessive ignorance and perverted love.

SELF–OTHER

The polarity of the sexes represents a self-other polarity too. In unfolding its young self a child quickly comes to acquire gender identity as a male or female. Later the intimacies of sexual love open deeper experiences of finding oneself in the loving embrace of the other, who is sufficiently different to mark off the boundaries of self and sufficiently alike to reinforce a common humanness. Only an adult sexuality in a true love relationship can match the infant-parent relationship in open inspections of body and spirit, in mutual contemplation and handling of the other's embodied self. As a mother mirrors the face of her child, so a lover reflects the face of the beloved. Finding his or her real self cherished and valued, each partner communicates to the other a recognition of value of the human person that infuses life with meaning. Thus enters spiritual reality—the perception of truth and value that makes life worth living, the sense that one matters even in one's imperfection, that one is alive and real even in one's mortality.

Without lovingness released into human relationship, we suffer a deep loneliness that drives us into madness.[9] In defense against that loneliness where we receive neither self nor other, we resort to polarization. Rather than preserve the tensions of agreement and difference, the similarities and dissimilarities of female and male sexuality, we either split them into opposing polarizations or substitute divisive politicizations for them.

THE THIRD DETOUR

If we cannot avoid splitting and sexual warfare by wiping out images of sexual polarity, what other solution is possible? Today it is often proposed to replace the old imagery of sexual polarity with a new one of human sexuality as androgynous. This image holds great appeal. It frees us from sexual stereotyping. It pictures the whole person as a blend of masculine and feminine characteristics. It emphasizes the role of cultural conditioning in forming gender identity. If we change our cultural images of male and female, the argument runs, we can condition our children toward a peace-bringing androgynous sexual model.

Several objections immediately come to mind. The first is, we must be careful not to replace one reductionism with another. We know the familiar Freudian slogan: "Anatomy is destiny." Is it any better to announce now that cultural conditioning is destiny? Is it any real improvement to assert that our male and female sexual identities arise solely from cultural influences on our gender formation? This view ignores the concrete reality of our bodies, which are predominantly male or female and remain the loci in which we live in the world. The body houses the spiritual, physical, psychological forces through which and by which we touch other people and are touched by them. Our body space does affect and shape us; but it does not altogether determine us. Our particular psyches, cultural backgrounds, and large symbolic inheritances of masculine and feminine images influence us decisively.

The androgynous view also ignores much else about the cultural images that condition us. These images are the means by which we think about fundamental matters of sexuality, gender, role formation, and every relationship between the sexes. They possess no immutable status nor do they exert exclusive deterministic effect on human identity, because the body and the psyche also exert their own kinds of formative influences. Cultural images can be changed by the intervention of consciousness, but it is a consciousness filled and formed by the very images it would alter. These images are created by the interplay of personal and social life, by inherited instinct and custom, by conscious and unconscious worlds of experience.

Discarding misused images does not save us from destructive

splits in ourselves. Discarding images serves only to erase part of our conscious humanity. As Jung puts it, "Concepts are coined and negotiable values; images are life."[10] We do not merely think about images: we think with them and by means of them. Images and the theories that emerge from them are part of what Karl Popper calls "World Three": "The fact that such theories are not bodies of impersonal facts about the world but are products of the human mind makes them personal achievements of an astonishing order."[11] Discarding those images of male and female, those symbols of masculine and feminine which have ordered human life for centuries, pushes us back into an imageless void, into the morass of unreflective unconscious process, without the aid of form-giving, order-creating symbols.

To say we cannot do without our images of the masculine and the feminine does not condemn us to use them only in their present forms. The images can change; indeed they must change and do, and we can sometimes hasten the change. But in our zeal to combat the discriminatory abuses of sexual polarity, we can fall into the fantasy that we can control all its imagery. On the one hand we regress to a presexual, nondifferentiated image of neither-nor androgynous unisex. On the other, we compensate for this regression with exaggerated emphasis on ego control. Our consciousness will somehow produce the images our unconscious has neglected. We will import feminine imagery where it has been lacking. All pronouns will now be he-she; the godhead will be referred to as Mother-Father, and so forth. We confine ourselves to ego plans and ego engineering and almost entirely lose touch with the expansive potentialities and organic growth of our unconscious mental processes. Ironically, we employ as solution the very attitude we have defined as the problem. We criticize the domination of masculine imagery and yet we caricature its worst expressions in this quick-fix mentality to make present what is absent. We get a conscious solution to a consciously defined problem; we do not get a new image that connects us to a newly unfolding reality. A change in grammar is not an adequate response to the exclusion of women and of the feminine in collective consciousness. We apply a remedy rather than participate in the organic growth of new images born from new mixtures of conscious and unconscious processes, from cultural and psychic influences, from women and men receiving all of themselves.

We must also object to the attempt to bypass human reality in this way of addressing the identity issue. If we adopt the image of androgyny as a literal description of human sexuality, we are almost bound to flee the concrete tasks of learning to live as men and women, to differentiate conflicting images within us, to integrate instinctual drives, and to harmonize the symbols that insist on proclaiming the masculine and feminine sides of ourselves.

Regression to a pre-Oedipal state where no firm differentiation exists between maleness and femaleness may offer relief from the tensions involved in achieving gender identity and relations to the other sex. In such a state (which can continue throughout one's life), ego-boundaries are fluid, sexual impulses blur with their opposites, love and hate merge. One appeal of bisexuality or of homosexuality as an alternative life-style is this easing of strain involved in attempting to achieve a discrete dominant identity as male or female. In place of composing a reliable identity as woman or man, and of finding and creating one's personal style of sexual identity, one can simply float, merge, blend, remain vague in outline. This state seems more flexible on the surface, but breaks down when intimacy is attempted with another person.

The image of androgyny turns into a dead end for women particularly. Once again the female and the symbolism of the feminine are skipped over. We used to be second-class citizens. Is the goal now "to be just the same as men"? Are we to move from the inferior sex to an androgynous creature without ever receiving and being received by others as the distinct female form of being human that we are? Is it progress to leap from the old repression of women to the new one that proclaims there is nothing distinctly feminine, no real difference from the masculine? Individual women need to be counted and taken account of, not as males, not as male surrogates, not as androgynous compilations, but as themselves, as present in their own particular way of being women, in their many ways, their many selves, their many different presences as women.

3

Relocating the Issue

We have seen that the three ways of attacking discrimination against women are too often detours that lead to dead ends. The first way is so fearful of the feminine that oppressive stereotypes about the woman's role are applied to actual female persons. The result is subtle and massive injustice against women in society. Here the fear of the female is dealt with by efforts to control the lives of women.

The second way seeks to avoid injustice to woman by attacking the images of sexual polarity and annihilating them. This way only represses from consciousness the fact of sexual difference and fosters an indulgence of rage when that which is repressed inevitably returns in displaced form. The third way seeks to avoid discrimination against women by regression to a presexual stage where no differentiation has yet occurred. This is overlaid with a pseudo consciousness that would control things with a fix-it mentality, an extreme opposite to the undifferentiated energies amassing in the unconscious.

All three ways avoid the feminine as distinct in its own right. All three ways reach dead ends because they fasten onto the problem at the wrong point. They focus on the image of sexual polarity as the cause of discrimination against women rather than on fear of the female and of what the feminine symbolizes.

The central question must be asked again and the origin of the problem located where it belongs. Must sexual polarity inevitably degenerate into hostile polarization of the sexes? Or is there an alternate path where perception of sexual difference promotes both differentiation of sexual identity and reciprocal and mutual relationships between the sexes? The answer to the first question is a firm no and to the second an unqualified yes. For the problem originates in projecting the image of sexual polarity instead of receiving it. We enter the problem at the point where the image ceases to be an image, where it flattens into a univocal reified label pasted on people. The problem originates not in the fact of sexual polarity *per se,* but in the projection of fears about it onto others. All of this amounts to an elaborate evasion, a way to avoid accepting the sexual polarity in oneself, particularly the fear of taking full possession of its feminine side. One person tries to manage this fear by depositing on women alone all feminine modalities of being and then assigning them inferior roles. Another denies this fear by trying to annihilate any distinction between masculine and feminine. A third seeks a regressive return to an unconscious state, the one that existed before awareness of the feminine made its claims.

To accept the feminine into full consciousness as a distinct cluster of symbolic images neither condones discrimination against women nor denies that images of the feminine will and must change. On the contrary, it means that at last we are giving up the ostrich position, hiding from sexual differences out of fear of the feminine. It means that we receive woman and the symbolism of the feminine associated with her.

Why is there such fear of the feminine? Because to both sexes woman represents, in a variety of ways, the presence of an otherness that cannot be controlled or manipulated. From the psychoanalytical point of view the female and the feminine convey the mysteries and threats of the unconscious as it confronts consciousness and sometimes invades it. The unconscious does not act rationally, but in random fashion from purposes of its own. It presents consciousness with a demanding "other" that must be reckoned with. The world of this other seems dark and mysterious, even alarming, to the world of consciousness which the ego strives to maintain. The ego's emergence from the unconscious is strikingly symbolized by a child's emergence into independence from its mother. The darkness of the womb, the dark feeling and mood, so closely associated with the unconscious, invest the female with that unmistakable sense of otherness that belongs to the unconscious.

From the point of view of our Judeo-Christian tradition, the soul has always been represented as female. Its mysteries, its flights, its patient flowering, its insistent bids for attention have again and again been likened to a woman's nature. As a result, the woman is endowed with the symbolic burden of being a link, an intercessor, a mediator to another world. The only female figure coming close to membership in the Godhead has been the divine intercessor—either as Sophia, the personification of wisdom, or as the compassionate Mother of God.

Depth psychologists of different schools amass evidence for the sexual polarity of human beings that supports and extends these ideas. Though different schools describe it in different terms, the point is usually the same.[1] Jung asserts that the whole person is contrasexual—a man consciously related to the feminine aspects of himself, a woman consciously in touch with her masculine side. Guntrip discusses male doing and female being, as modes of human reality existing in each sex. Winnicott writes of the pure female element as a being that precedes doing and the pure male element as the doing that spontaneously flows from being. Both elements belong to each sex. Bakan writes of the same polarity as a set of tendencies toward communion and toward agency. These terms appeal to Chodorow, who traces the cultural influences of child-rearing that help shape these identifications. Both Bakan and Chodorow argue for the inclusion of both tendencies in each sex. Jean Baker Miller describes affiliative and competitive styles of apprehending reality, styles that each sex develops. Melanie Klein traces the similarities and differences in the formation of a girl's and a boy's identities, a perception of differences that facilitates perception of traits held in common. Each child must come to terms with matriarchal and patriarchal ego-identification and superego components.

On the basis of such diverse evidence for sexual polarity we must ask why we have not received it gladly into consciousness, instead of splitting the polarity apart into hostile roles assigned to each sex? What would be the significance of receiving this fact now—in this time of heightened awareness of sexual identity?

The point is that projection, not reception, has been our dominant response to sexual differences. The problem of discrimination against women originates in the mechanism of projection; we throw out of ourselves as individuals onto women as a collectivity those elements of being, symbolized as feminine, that we deeply fear in ourselves. The woman who would receive all of herself and be received by others hands these projections back to us. She acknowledges both the masculine and feminine elements in herself, strongly claiming them as her own, and will not project them onto others if she can help it. She makes us confront our own projections, bringing us to a decisively new threshold of awareness. For the significance of receiving instead of projecting focuses on the implosion into consciousness of energy heretofore distributed anarchically around us. When we withdraw projections, all the energy they carry returns to us. The implosion of energy can either unseat a fragile ego or cause a radical deepening and widening of consciousness from which a fresh new perception of human nature may arise. We may envision a man or a woman firmly containing sexual polarity, a vital being with a clear hold on identity, whether female or male, and with conscious relation to the opposite sexual aspects which each contains. Such a person radiates a concrete, authoritative, receiving presence, open to all facets of being. To reach this threshold of being we need to grasp thoroughly the mechanism of projection.

PROJECTION AS DEFENSE AND DIFFERENTIATION

Projection occurs in all of us as a normal psychic function of defense and differentiation. I stress this fact at the outset to defeat any temptation to lecture ourselves or others to stop projecting. By definition, projection occurs unconsciously and happens *to* us; we only discover it when we find ourselves doing it.

Projection always occurs as an initial state of the breakup of the unconscious identity of self with another. Projection is one of our earliest and most persistent psychic mechanisms, by which we defend our egos against unconscious impulses, affects, and perceptions that we fear will prove painful if admitted into full awareness. We deny consciousness to these internal elements, eject them from the psyche, and perceive them as originating outside ourselves. Psychic contents that in fact originate in ourselves we see as originating in someone else. We expel from consciousness aspects of ourselves that belong to us but of which we are largely unconscious. At the same time we ascribe ownership of them to other persons or to causes external to ourselves. To some degree we treat the other person as a blank screen onto which we can cast various aspects of our personalities that we somehow cannot yet consciously acknowledge.

Such a defense shields us against recognizing disturbing elements in ourselves that might break up a state of unconscious unity with another. It spares us the pain of recognizing our own ambivalent emotions as one source of conflict within us. For example, in marriage we may want to hold on to the harmonious relationship that existed before serious disagreements arose. By seeing our partner as the cause of tension, we can persuade ourselves that if only he or she would change, harmony would be restored. We thereby protect our own self-image as good, free of negative reactions and troublesome attitudes. We do so by projecting the bad in ourselves onto someone else. The pressure of work, for example, might be held as an excuse for problems inside the marriage. In the case of wife-beating we see projection working in its most primitive form. There the husband projects onto the wife fearful impulses in himself that he violently repudiates. He then punishes her for having them while indulging these impulses in himself in the beating process.

More commonly, men project onto women feminine aspects of themselves along with their unconscious expectation that the female will manage these parts of life for them. Many marriage problems begin when a woman refuses to carry such projections. A major thrust of the woman's movement points women toward recognizing themselves as persons, no longer to be defined in the images men project onto them.

By locating disturbing elements outside ourselves, we try to avoid the painful awareness of life's ambiguities. We all possess mixed emotions, frightening impulses to hate as well as to love. Moreover, we cannot unload them on other persons. Recognizing our own ambivalence brings painful loss of the antecedent unitary innocence, a once-serene state of harmony in ourselves and toward others. We cannot be either all good or all evil (some people, like criminal personalities, project all good onto others). We exist as mixtures of good and evil.

Projection always occurs when a state of unconscious identity of self and other begins to break up. Projection is a halfway point between unconscious and conscious awareness of those parts of ourselves we need to recognize. We see them first in the face of our neighbor before we accept that face as a mirror of our own.

We try to avoid conflict by laying the evil (or good) at our neighbor's door while retaining the good (or evil) image for ourselves. This defensive function exerts an initially positive effect. Projection helps us begin to distinguish good from evil. We lump together all our own bad impulses to attack, to devour, to chop up and disembowel, and all our bad feelings of being left empty, abandoned, and frustrated. We gather all this into one overwhelming bundle. We thus form an identifiable image of badness. With an economy of effort we want to put all that onto someone else. We arrive at images of goodness in a similar way. Before we can imagine ways to reconcile badness and goodness we need to establish clear images of each. Hence the appeal of old-fashioned cowboy movies with their simpleminded good-guy, bad-guy polarization, reflecting our earliest images of good and evil and permitting us to cheer lustily for the triumph of good.

In sexual matters projection initially helps us distinguish between things masculine or feminine. In growing up both consciously and unconsciously we gather loosely defined images of the feminine from our experiences with women, our perceptions of their behavior, our feelings about them, our response to the female body, and what our culture tells us about female heroines, villains, goddesses, and historical figures, well known and obscure. Boys seeking a masculine self-image, initially project this feminine content onto all the females they meet, thereby demarking the male's psychological territory from the female's. The boy's difficulty in making his first claims to identity center on seeing himself as separate from the mother, that original harbor of being, that authority, that body and soul. The girl's difficulty in securing her own identity as female centers on finding her own place within her identification with her mother, a likeness that does not swallow up her distinct individuality.

Sexual stereotypes occur in a less differentiated stage of consciousness where masculine and feminine sometimes must be sharply demarked in order to be secured; differentiation of the sexes is a step toward envisioning persons who consciously and happily include masculine and feminine elements in their being. A man needs a firm ego-identity before he can integrate feminine components into his identity. Where such firm differentiation fails to occur, resort to stereotypes usually happens instead, creating a sort of pseudo differentiation, a fixing onto outer appearance, because of lack of secure hold on the real thing within.

At the present time in some parts of our world we seem collectively to be moving beyond these stereotypes to a more inclusive consciousness of sexual polarity. Women repudiate their identification with projected contents of the feminine. Many persons of both sexes seek an androgynous image. In some cases sexual polarity is itself rejected. All these signs may be interpreted as attempts to move across a new threshold of consciousness into a wholeness that recognizes and puts together, in all their individual variations, male and female elements in persons. Stereotypes that may initially facilitate distinctions between the masculine and the feminine eventually cripple such awareness.

We can be sure a projection of a stereotyped image is at work in us whenever we insist on an unvarying specifically defined nature for the female or male. With such projecting, we may be trying to establish who we are by labeling who we are not or by trying to say *that* is who we are. Or we may be registering the first disturbing signs that we need to assimilate those contents we want to unload onto our neighbor of the opposite sex. Projecting sexual contents that we need to integrate prevents us from achieving more consciousness. What may initially help us to distinguish who we are, if held on to too long, impedes our learning who we actually are. Such projecting pollutes the psychic atmosphere. We simply put out there what we shun in here, inside ourselves. Projection used in this extremely defensive manner almost inevitably fuels social oppression. We hound, persecute, and look with contempt on persons who carry parts of ourselves we cannot accept. We scorn in them what we do not own in ourselves. Or we may project onto them the good qualities in ourselves that we cannot receive as our own; we insist the other act out the idealized role we attribute to them. It is precisely here that we may see the second function of projection—to help us perceive and become conscious of what is really there in the other person and what is present in ourselves.[2]

PROJECTION AS PERCEPTION

Sooner or later we notice that we are caught in projection. Though we may not know the word itself in its technical sense, we know all too well the signs that projection is operating in us. We feel highly agitated about some quality in another person, whether the agitation is excessive admiration or condemnation. We cannot leave the issue alone, but must rehearse it in our minds over and over, writing still another letter, consulting still another friend about it. We feel compelled to get to the bottom of the terribly troublesome issue. It is like a modern tar baby—the more we poke at it, the more we are stuck in it. The reason we cannot leave the issue alone is that we have dumped on another person part of our own psychology that really belongs to us. If we can observe the agitation, the compulsive emotional show, the obsessive behavior, we can finally sense our identification with this trait in the other. Thus getting caught in this projection can aid us to become more conscious.

Consciousness enlarges us in two principal ways. We notice, to begin with, that the person upon whom we project really differs considerably from the images we attribute to him or her. That particular person's presence simply does not match the images with which we endow him or her. This applies even if the other person does in fact possess some aspects of those images. For we still feel inextricably mixed up with aspects of the other person. In sharp contrast to other faults or virtues, this particular set of traits gets under our skin, drives us wild, in fact, indicating by the agitation aroused in us that some projection of our own psyche is involved. In that way the reality of the person out there rejects our projected images and stands forth in its own right, demanding that we take accurate notice of it. But secondly, that part of our own psyche—that special content, largely of our own making, in the image we have been projecting—also demands our attention and a conscious relationship to it.

We need to take notice of what this content is—what sort of image, of affect, and of emotional and behavioral reactions we ascribe to the other person and how that in some way really does belong to us. It is part of ourselves that seeks entrance into our consciousness and asks to be assimilated to our own identities. Take, for example, images projected onto women. Stereotyped ones concern the body, sexual impulses, and irrational emotionality. For a man to notice this sort of projected content means that he is beginning to ask himself where his body needs, sexual desires, and wild emotions must be clearly recognized and attached to his own identity. He needs to ask where he is outlawing his own vulnerabilities and need for protection, by putting it all onto some woman in his life whom he will protect. Or, to take a more pathological example, where a man shudders with revulsion at the image or the odor of the female genitals, he must ask where he has endowed female parts with what he fears as a terrible dark hole in himself, some primeval and fetid place that threatens to swallow him up.

Some of the more deeply disturbed behavior of women also contains elements of projection onto men. They brand all men as rapists at heart, as scheming, power-mad bullies seeking only to subjugate women. A woman must ask where in her psychology an inner tyrannous attacker exists, one who criticizes her every move toward independence and self-esteem. To recognize such an inner tyrant does not deny outer actual social or legal discrimination against women. Recognizing projections and withdrawing them is not a panacea for evils that exist in the world. But it is much easier to fight those real evils if one is not simultaneously endowing them with fantasies of persecution. For then an evil of large enough dimensions is magnified into a monstrous fantasy imbued with the nightmarish qualities of one's early childish fears. One must then conduct an impossible fight on two fronts at once—outwardly against a recognizable injustice, inwardly against the terrors of the unconscious.

WITHDRAWING AND INTEGRATING PROJECTIONS

When we notice the existence of two realities, of person and of image, we initiate the process of withdrawing projection. This in turn produces its own startling multiple effects. One of first importance is social. We withdraw psychic pollution from the atmosphere. We soften up. We are less apt unconsciously and compulsively to hound a person we now recognize to have been carrying this unfavored part of ourselves. We lessen our need to control those on whom we imposed parts of ourselves that we needed to control in ourselves. Women, relieved of the burden of carrying a man's need for nurturing, no longer feel threatened by accusations of disordered femininity when they develop their ambition and aggression. There is less unconscious coercion to keep women "in their place," usually a repository for qualities and virtues that find no place in a society dedicated to competition and success. Women are less apt to be assigned the roles of guardians of the virtues and keepers of the softer finer things of life that have been excluded from the marketplace. Now each person must reckon with this quality and find conscious relation to it as part of his or her own personality.

The increase of consciousness that follows withdrawal of projection means a decrease in the repression that fuels social oppression. Jesus himself counseled against this rejection of parts of our selves, both sexual and sinful, in his parable of the stoning of the adulterous woman. He showed the men who would stone the woman that they could not rid themselves of their feminine side by projecting its "badness" onto a prostitute. What they wanted to stone in her belonged to each of them and needed to be accepted and faced. The woman also had to face her own sin, but only that, not the accumulated deformities of the crowd. When we deny less of what belongs to us, we need less to find a scapegoat on whom we can dump all the unwanted parts of ourselves. We begin to clean up our own backyard. Instead of splitting the poles of sexual polarity into reified polarized roles projected onto each sex, we can look at the projected images to find where they belong in ourselves.

Projections by their nature are unconscious and thus primitive and impersonal. Hence it is not always immediately evident where the parts of ourselves projected onto others belong in our own psyches. But belong they do. A good test is to list in simple fashion what we see in the other that gets such a rise out of us. "I hate in so-and-so these things"—then we list the characteristics, ostensibly in the other, that we find so offensive. Or, if the other commands our unbounded admiration, then we list the characteristics that evoke such respect or affection in us. Similarly in relation to the opposite sex, we should list those qualities that arouse immediate attraction and those that demand immediate repudiation. Then put all the lists away for a day. Return to them, erase the other person's name and insert our own. There we will find a list of our own qualities that need conscious development. Where there are faults, they belong to us in some way, not necessarily in exactly the same way we spy them in our neighbor, but in some version in us that demands conscious attention and effort to claim them. Where there are virtues, they too belong in some way to us, summoning our every effort to develop them by establishing conscious connection to them.

In relation to the opposite sex, we will discover a gathering of qualities in such a list that sketches a rudimentary image of the opposite pole of sexual polarity as it exists in our own psychology. That kind of man is for me a conveyor of the masculine—composed of the influences of men in my own past and present life, images of the male in my particular culture, symbols of the masculine that have become active for me in my interchanges with others and with unconscious aspects of myself. That image of woman is what I have projected onto females, expecting them to carry and contain for me; that is what I must come to terms with as the concrete feminine aspects of my own personality.

A man who dreams he opens the door to a crazed woman bursting with aggressive feelings, one who simply demands to be admitted, confronts a part of his own feminine nature that feels left out and a little crazed for being thus excluded. She—his feminine side—is not just passively bemoaning her fate, but rather is aggressively doing something about it. So the dreamer reflecting on the dream feels mixed reactions. On the one hand he does not much care for her agitated state, but on the other he recognizes something good about her aggression. She does not just withdraw and mope, but actively stands up for her feelings and wants him to receive them too. In fact, she did in the dream what the dreamer realizes he needs to do in his life—to notice when he feels left out and hurt by being overlooked and to stand with those feelings, whether based on real exclusion by others or not. The dream girl shows in personified form precisely what his ego needs to become aware of—that when he feels overlooked he tends to react in an angry, aggressive way, enough out of proportion to the cause to appear a little crazed. The remedy for this hurt is precisely to accept those vulnerable feelings and aggressively support them. In other words, by acknowledging his hurt he joins his aggressive energies to his vulnerable side instead of covering up his pain by angry bluster. What is recovered to consciousness then is both his softer vulnerability and his tougher aggressive self-assertion and self-support. This does not mean he should behave as the dream-girl did, acting full of demands and huffiness. She gives him in primitive form the valuable connections between his hurt and his anger that his ego can now refine. If instead of receiving this feminine part of himself, the dreamer simply projects it onto some woman in his life, he might see her as crazy, impossibly demanding, and intrusive. His only defense is to label her as an aggressive bitch. Or if inwardly his ego identifies with this feminine part of himself, and he behaves in this angry, crazy way himself, he would simply produce puzzlement in his hearers at the very least, and more likely their rejection and withdrawal.

To receive into consciousness this noisy girl as part of his own psychology is difficult indeed. But it would immediately benefit his relation to the woman in his life, who would no longer be pressed into carrying this part of himself for him. He would achieve a personal link to the world of the opposite sex through conscious connection to the feminine side of himself. When confronting an actual woman bursting with hurt and angry demands he would possess some immediate understanding for her because he knew these feelings in himself. Reaching the world of the other sex within one goes a long way toward building a sense of our common human identity. Opponents of the images of sexual polarity fear that emphasis upon it will foster more divisions between men and women. On the contrary, perceptions of difference make experience of similarity possible. Receiving this noisy girl as part of his own psychology changes the dreamer's relation to his own vulnerability. He accepts its presence happily and learns how to protect it and nurture it in a way that will bring it into relationship instead of covering it up in some unconscious expectation that the other person will take care of it.

Withdrawing projections from others means we cease obscuring their reality by seeing them only as carriers of parts of ourselves. The nature of the other as other opens up to us. We perceive the one who is there. We may now receive the concrete presence of persons in their idiosyncratic reality, instead of, for example, stamping all women from the same mold of our unconscious projections.

A second effect of withdrawal of projection is a great implosion of energy returning to our own psyche that we must now claim. The man of our example must somehow receive the image of an aggressive girl as his own, which means a radical alteration in his own self-image. To take her seriously as a part of himself means to change his masculine identity. It is no longer all-male; now there is a feminine component as well. For a woman to withdraw her projection onto men of an image of aggressive tyranny means she must find where she needs consciously to develop her own aggression and to claim it. Otherwise it will run unconsciously through projections, trampling tyrannically on herself and others. Her ego must expand to receive this aggressive component as part of her conscious picture of herself. If she accuses men of constant prejudice against women, making them second-class citizens, fit only to attend to children and cook meals, she must now ask herself how and where this picture of femininity belongs to her. Where does she need to make conscious connection to her own (unconscious) image of woman as a second-class citizen? What has made these images so negative? Where does something in her scorn the large possibilities in her own body and spirit? This interceding consciousness may save her from the twin compulsion either to adopt the roles of mother and wife with a kind of violence, or automatically to repudiate them.[3] Receiving these personal factors into her consciousness helps her to make a personal choice, arrived at for specific reasons and out of particular feelings, in the concrete circumstances of her life.

Examples are countless. A woman may project onto a man the qualities of a supportive, loving father she never had. Eventually she must claim this supportive energy for herself in herself, lest she remain a sort of father's daughter all her life, transferring to teacher, to employer, to preacher, to political figure, or whomever, this dynamic image she feels so much in need of. To recover a conscious connection to this support entirely within herself would free her from a fixed daughter role, free her to claim a secure inner authority, and to grow up into full womanhood.

A woman may see men as weak, frightened of her intensity, easily blown over, always interpreting her actions and attitudes as demanding. She fears the man will retreat into silent withdrawal if she lets all of her passion show, whether sexual passion, excitement about her career or a political issue, or just great élan about being alive. She will view him then as of dubious sexuality, uncertain in his own feeling life, apt to crumble. She needs to find where within herself she turns away from her own intensity instead of embracing it, where she retreats into noncommunicative silence instead of affirming what she feels. Where, she must ask herself, does she doubt that her intense passion is entirely feminine. Why can she not accept it as containable and confirming of her identity as a woman? Where does she back off from her own excitement as a sexual being? This habit of absence and doubt about herself may have been tutored by her father, or brother, or implanted cultural images of the female. But now these attitudes live in her, as part of her own makeup and reflection about herself. Saying that the attitudes arise from cultural conditioning may help locate their source for her but will offer no solution. She may have caught the infection from her father but the infection now is in her system and she must deal with it.

Projection onto someone of the opposite sex comprises one of life's great experiences, touching our body, our emotions, our spirit. It reaches into our past, rearranges and often breaks the grip of parental images upon us, like the fairy-tale knight who takes the princess away from her father's castle. Such an experience opens up a future we dared not contemplate, making us feel alive and real with the courage to be ourselves in ways we never experienced before. In the positive modes of projection we talk of falling wildly, deeply in love, totally pulled out toward the other person, and pulled into our soul and the whole world now opening to us. We feel summoned to step out from peripheral cares toward essential things, to be the self we really are, to dare what we believe. Like characters in a fairy tale, we win through hard tasks to reach our beloved; we journey many miles to free our true love from bondage to the witch, from imprisonment in the form of animals, from a deathlike unconsciousness. In finding the other we find ourself. Even in its negative forms projection onto the opposite sex compromises an unforgettable experience. We feel in thrall, powerless before the other, plunged recklessly onto a destructive course, drawn like a moth to flame where our soul is threatened with annihilation. In losing the other we fear to lose ourself.

Either way, positively or negatively, something important is opening in ourselves to ourselves, especially if we take the time and effort to go with the energy inward, whether or not we can pursue an outer relationship with another person. In positive projection we are tempted to live relationship out in outer form alone. The one advantage of negative projection, of unhappy love affairs, is that they force us for our own survival to try to understand what really happened. In either case the inward challenge is the same, a call to come into conscious knowledge of the primordial images of the opposite sex that have been stirred in us. This means not only recalling the formative images of the opposite sex from our own biographies—images of mother, sister, teacher, and others, images drawn from culture and our heritage. It means more. It means discovering which archetypal themes of the other sex are alive in us, which forces in us comprise the opposite, less conscious sides of our personalities, elements that bring to the surface with them great chunks of unconscious life to which we need to establish conscious connection. Here sexual images touch on their complementary spiritual components. For example, in a woman's psychology the image of the masculine often may personify an authoritative word, or a potent force for truth. One woman dreamed that at the end of a rocky deserted road in a barren landscape a fierce figure of a man awaited her arrival. He was a man like a prophet in the wilderness, not evil, but imbued with so much power of spirit that he was fearsome and there was no way she could go around him or avoid him. Whether or not such images of the masculine belong to all women, they lived in this particular dreamer and she had to come to terms with them if she wanted to receive all of herself.

The key is consciousness. Our awareness widens and deepens to receive missing parts of ourselves, those that we used to project onto other people. All the psychic energy bound up in the images of the opposite sex returns to us then. If we receive it warmly, our consciousness opens to the unconscious origins of images that must be looked at for themselves, in their own terms, with their own rights. Each person thus embarks on the adventure of discovering what the symbols and traditions of the masculine and the feminine mean to him or her specifically. Identity springs loose from imprisoning conformity to abstract categories. We see now that we can fashion our identities ourselves, personally, in relation to other persons, to traditions, and to symbols that we recognize as they act in potent ways deep within ourselves.

Although withdrawing projections makes us more softly receptive to others, it also makes our consciousness tougher in relation to ourselves and our psychic tasks. The withdrawal of projection makes us notice the existence of the real sexual polarity within ourselves. We can discover how our own feminine and masculine elements combine to make up who we are as we reach out to receive all of them.

Rather than falling into hostile images of sexual polarization or returning to earlier versions of a presexual androgyny, now we see persons as they actually are, in all their differences. We see the particular images that inhabit us and we are not frightened or depressed or in any way put off by them. An outer world of otherness opens up to us as we open to it. We receive gratefully and as fully our own an inner world of the unconscious that has often seemed so impossibly other to the ways of the conscious ego. We can avoid the crippling force of disjunctive sexual roles and the dismal power struggles between the sexes, for we recognize now that both sexual modalities belong to both sexes. Out of this new consciousness our imaginations are challenged to create new images of masculine-feminine polarity, images more adapted to the currents of our own times perhaps than those we have inherited, and with them new combinations of personal identity more alive with our own life in them. It is that full coming to terms with the feminine and masculine elements of our being which is the subject of our next chapters.

4

Receiving the Feminine Elements of Being

Feminine elements of being both attract us and arouse a deep-seated fear in us. We combat the fear with the weapon of hatred. Projecting these elements of being onto women, we seek to control them by keeping "women in their place." Women's struggle and the symbolism of the feminine have everything to do with the mystery of being, with what it means to be entirely human. Hence they have everything to do with a religious point of view. We must ask why these elements of being are so closely associated with females and feminine symbolism. We must describe what these elements are. We must ask why fear and projection promote hate and tyranny. Then we must ask what social and theological changes would occur if we tried to face those elements of being more directly.

WHY FEMININE?

Why should these elements of being be associated with the female? Why should they be called feminine? Why not just human? There are several good answers. First, our primary experience with them begins with our mothers. We are born of women; we partake of female flesh; we emerge from female bodies which produce food to nourish us. Our mothers are the first to bond with us psychologically. They are preoccupied with our coming into the world and with our nascent being in the first months of life.[1]

To be flesh of another's flesh—a phrase the Bible uses to connote the deepest intimacies of love—affects who we are and what we become at levels far below consciousness. This feminine element of being has to do with more than our birth. It effects our being alive, being a person, rather than just passively existing. The female element of being links us inextricably with our experience of being a distinct "I," one bodily and emotionally present, one awaited, recognized, and greeted over the early years of life, one with a capacity to see others as distinctly there and persons themselves in their own right.

Secondly, until very recently Western culture has emphasized the role of woman as mother and nurturer of children. Thus most of us still associate coming into being or failing to do so with the women who took care of us or neglected us. We may now want to alter this cultural tradition, but we cannot avoid its impact on how we perceive our passage from dependency and how we apprehend ourselves and others. Just as we are born out of a specific female body, we are born into particular cultural systems that help to shape our perceptions of self and world. To change those basic systems we must first see them clearly and grasp all the meaning we can concerning a range of inchoate experience at the base of our being.

Thirdly, strongly associated with the feminine is a large cluster of images, emotional and behavioral reactions, that convey to us a strong life of their own.[2] The origins of these symbols cannot be traced solely to objects introjected or implanted from without. The argument against this position, that such a range of feminine symbols merely demonstrates a sexism that overarches the centuries, appeals mainly because of its stunning simplemindedness. Reductionism on such a grand scale is an unconscious tribute to male power; it merely offers escape from the hard fact that the feminine element of being has been recognized for centuries. We may challenge the way it has been misused to abuse women, but we cannot avoid it or reject it. Instead, we must recover to individual and collective consciousness what the feminine means, both concretely and symbolically.

Concretely, the feminine refers to the personal and collective life of women—all women—women of different races, cultures, colors, ages, single or married, with or without children. We do not all have the same needs or the same expectations. Our goals vary. We do not have the same economic or cultural backgrounds. We do not have the same education. Women differ among themselves. We must make room for the differences.

Symbolically the feminine comprises the vast world of imagery people have consciously or unconsciously associated with women from the beginning of time. These images of the feminine transcend individual lives and particular cultures or historical eras. Some images of the feminine at this symbolic level help us greatly. They encompass and delineate certain splits we have suffered in society. Next to the white Madonna with the Christ-child is the black Madonna of Montserrat or Einsiedeln. Next to the figures of the good nurturing mother is the dark figure of the witch. Next to the image of the Madonna with the newborn Christ-child suckling at her breast is the image—placed in our liturgical calendar only three days after Christmas—of all those other mothers crying without consolation because of the Slaughter of the Innocents.

This world of images is not the same as the world of our shared daily existence with each other, nor is it traceable solely to objects introjected from that world. It is not the same as our private unconscious life and it is not reducible to projections of the instincts. This world of images lies somewhere among all these areas, living a role as our adult version of the playtime of our nursery years with beloved toys.[3] Our symbol systems, along with other cultural realities—what Cassirer calls the "spiritual organs" of culture, meaning art, language, theology, science—create for us a transitional space between our private inner world and the outer world we share with others. In this space between worlds, our symbols possess a reality of the same order as the favorite toy that possesses a name, a personality, and reflects back to the child experience of union of self and world, a function the child's mother originally provided. Similarly our symbols possess their distinct existence and mirror back to us the face of who we are in our essential personhood. The toy defines the boundaries of the union between the individuating child and the mother, filling the ever-growing space between them as the child unfolds an increasingly independent identity. Similarly our symbols mark a sphere of union between our human existence and being at its source, in the manifold varieties of ways we experience and picture that source. It is in this space between worlds, between inner and outer, that symbols of the feminine exist and perform a mirroring function, reflecting back to us our apprehension of a major modality of human existence.

Images of the feminine bespeak their own long tradition. One traditional symbol, for example, has been the all-inclusive goal of wholeness of being. This contrasts with a linear goal that allows even valuable fragments of being to fall away in the movement toward perfection. Women often receive projections of what men —and women who mimic them—think must be included in their world to make human life more complete.

In my experience as a minister years ago, I found that the kinds of services people asked me to do, in contrast to what they asked of the male senior minister, the classes they wanted me to teach, focused on the embarrassing gaps between what the congregation wanted to believe and what in fact it did believe. These good people were projecting the things they needed to have brought into consciousness onto me, to bring to some fulfillment. This kind of projection was no doubt influenced by my particular personality, and that of the congregation. Other women would have constellated other things. But it was clearly women who drew the projections of what had been left out of the religious life that needed to be included. Each of us comes with a specific presence. Each evokes different things. But in all, certain collective images of the feminine operate. We must know this and be conscious of it so that we can protect ourselves, neither falling into identification with the projections nor repudiating them outright. They express central realities and basic needs.

Fear of these elements of being lies behind hatred of the female. Right now, women and the symbolism of the feminine act as carriers of this issue of being, which accounts for its central connection to religious tradition. We find these elements in the Judeo-Christian faith, which in a fundamental way can provide a liberating place for women. But where our religious tradition falls away from its own center of being, it limits women, discouraging their insights, restricting the offices they can fill, pressuring them to imitate men rather than to bring their own particular presence into the church, tempting them with an image of androgyne that omits any specific female presence.

FEMININE ELEMENTS OF BEING

What then are these fearful elements of being? In my book *The Feminine in Jungian Psychology and in Christian Theology*, I considered many of the archetypal images that express the feminine modality of being human.[4] From entirely different perspectives, come similar concepts of what D. W. Winnicott, and Harry Guntrip after him, call the "female element of being."[5] Their research provides empirical data from early childhood that fleshes out the symbolic meaning of Jung's theory of archetypes. From these quite different directions, the focus on the feminine gathers intensity. Here I will focus on the three aspects of this female element of being that Winnicott discusses, all of them observable in a child's earliest experiences with a mother. I would add that these three elements form a basis for any significant experience in its birth and growing phases. They are: being as being-at-the-core-of-oneself, being as beginning by being-one-with another, and being as possessed of a personal continuity.

Associated with the feminine element in all of us is a sense of being-at-the-core-of-oneself. This involves a capacity to be, to be there calmly, at rest, sensing one's "self" as somehow found, given, and reflected, instead of achieved, created, or manufactured. Winnicott and Guntrip investigate the origins of this experience in the first months of life in the intimate mother-child relationship. There the mother acts as a mirror for her infant, reflecting back in her responses the child's being-there. The most ordinary games a parent plays with a child illustrate this crucial responsiveness to the child's being. When the mother plays identifying games with the child, pointing out, "This is your nose and this is your ear," the child can look into the mother's face and find reflected there its own face. Looking into the mother's face that is looking back, the infant discovers a sense of its own personal being. Here unfolds for the first time a child's capacity to feel alive, real, possessed of unique personal existence.

Being-at-the-core, then, means being vulnerable. We discover this essential "I am" experience, as Winnicott puts it, through our dependence on another person seeing and reflecting back to us the fact that "we are." The foundation of our capacity to be lies in the initial mother-child relationship, though it is not limited to that. That relationship gives us our first taste of being-at-the-core in any significant experience.

Being must accrue to us in each of our important relationships, not only with other people but also in all our experiences of the world, of symbols and ideas, of God. In each experience we initially find our being through its being reflected back to us by another. We depend on that; we are totally vulnerable to its presence or absence. Surprisingly, a successful dependence yields not a fixation but a full-bodied sense of individual being rooted at the core, a center that exists for oneself.

The Old Testament asserts the awesome numinous impact of such being-at-the-core in the revelation of God as "I am who I am." David Holbrook finds the same connection between dependent vulnerability and achieving being-at-the-core in Christian images: "the female element of being is the capacity to perceive the world, to love, and to develop symbols and a sense of richness in union—that which is meant by all the paintings in the world of Virgin and child—the capacity to be, to be alone, relying on inner resources." Holbrook argues that our failure to find ourselves vulnerable in this primary sense deprives us of an "inner core of stillness," a deprivation that acts as the root of alienation in our culture. Our hate originates here "in protest at being deprived of love," of that reflecting love which enables us to consent to be.[6]

A second major characteristic of the feminine element of being grows from an experience of being-at-one-with that precedes our being able to exist as individuals and also precedes "doing" of any kind. At first there is no distinction between a me and a not-me; at first we find our being in "quietness and an inexplicit togetherness" inaugurated in the mother-child relationship.[7] An ordinary "good-enough" mother, as Winnicott puts it, acts as a creative mirror returning to her child an image of being which the child, in turn, finds within through the mother having seen it. I would add that this fundamental at-one-ness preceding any sense we may have of a separate self occurs in other significant experiences too. I will deal with three: religion, love, and therapy.

The sense of "I am" created by togetherness dwells at the heart of religious experience. The Christian doctrine of atonement points to our finding the mystery of our being reflected back to us in the figure of Jesus Christ.[8] He reaches across our broken-apart-being into our counterfeit lives to reestablish us at the core where we find God's being-at-one-with us. Prior to the development of what Tillich called our "new being," we discover our true faces mirrored in Christ. Thus Julian of Norwich, the fourteenth-century mystic, writes of Christ "our mother" who knits us into God, giving birth to us in the spirit.[9] In our tacit dwelling in Christ we find the being we had lost hold of. This joyous stabilizing experience should make us realize why religion used sadistically is one of the worst of destructive instruments. Instead of finding a Christ who binds our wounds at the very core of our self, we are exhorted by a Christ who hectors us endlessly about what we should be doing. Such religion acts as a weapon directed against our vulnerable state of being, a tool of hate.

Another example of at-one-ness occurs in intense love relations. A direct connection extends between the feminine element of being, which is concerned with feeling alive and real, and what happens in a committed and loving sexual relationship. There we work directly on being. We are opened and seen in a total way comparable only to our earliest relation with a loving mother, or to a profound religious experience. We are exposed for what we are—with foibles, faults, possibilities, talents, beauties, imperfections—in the flesh, without disguise or hiding. We are inspected. Mirrored back in the face of the lover, we discover our true image. The depth of this encounter accounts for the devastating impact of a failed love affair. There we feel struck down at the core of our being. We feel cheated, denied, abused in our vulnerable center of being. Having first been seen as we are, we are suddenly playing roles with which the other has invested us. Sometimes the wound is so great, we vow never again to risk a love that makes us so vulnerable.

Another way in which people come strongly upon this basic experience of at-one-ness is in therapy. In all the different reasons people seek therapy there lies a common hope—to find a true self that has been lost in neurotic disturbances or crushed in psychotic disorder. Regardless of theoretical standpoint, therapists join in recognizing the invaluable right of the person to be a person. In short, therapy is a collaboration of persons who believe in the priceless value of the true human self. The therapist repeatedly reflects back the self the patient brings to the sessions. Such being-at-one-with the vulnerable core of the patient's being lies at the basis of all successful treatment.

The mirroring of the true self that happens in therapy sometimes happens in a startling way between our conscious ego and the unconscious. Our ego-identity is seen and reflected back to us through the figures of the unconscious that face us in our dreams. These "others" may lead us to that central experience of beholding objectively our subjective experience, the integrating center of the psyche that Jung calls the self. The paradox confounds us. We feel seen by a greater subject that exists objectively within us and thus confers objectivity on our subjective existence. The familiar divisions of subject and object coalesce and the hard-and-fast lines of consciousness dissolve in this experience.

We can understand, therefore, why we fear all these kinds of experiences of being-at-one-with. In these experiences consciousness tends to dissolve into degrees of intense identification of self with other. Even to contemplate such a dissolution of ego boundaries makes us feel dissociated, for we reenter modes of experience that lie beneath our achieved distinctions of me and not-me. There, to be means to be-at-one-with.

Fear of the Female

This sort of knowing by identifying with something, so central to the feminine element of being, accounts for one of the major reasons the female is hated: behind the hate lurks a tremendous fear of losing our conscious standpoint, our distinct me-ness. The threat is of a total loss of individuality resulting from the creative regression to being-at-one-with the other. In therapy, for example, we fear the incursions of craziness. Men who come to terms with their own feminine element, what Jung calls the anima, know the unsettling nature of this fear. The anima confronts a man's ego with an entirely different way of viewing himself and his world. At first, it seems to a man that his view and "hers" (the anima's) stand irrevocably opposed. To consider "her" view fills a man with dread that he may have to sacrifice his hard-won conscious value system. From this dread may spring a need to see the feminine as entirely secondary, inferior, less stable than the masculine. If a man remains unconscious of his fear of the feminine element in his own being he may compulsively act it out by projecting its threat onto actual females. From such projected fears spring some of the most hostile attitudes and prejudicial acts against women.

One man's dream illustrates the unnerving effect an anima figure may exert on a masculine self-image. The man appeared in his dream much as he saw himself in real life, focused and purposeful as he came to his therapy session, ready to work. But in the dream, unhappily, he was kept waiting by the therapist, who had first to attend to a wan, pale, girl-woman who seemed neglected and unwell. She had worms under her hair which she had attempted to wash and brush into some sort of presentable appearance. While the therapist put the girl to bed and tended to her wormy hair, the man was caught in conflicting emotions. He saw that the girl needed immediate and caring attention, yet it was his hour and he was impatient to get on with his session.

The dream depicts two conflicting views: the man's—the dream-ego's—readiness to move ahead and the anima's faintness and need of care because of which the man must wait. Neither view is necessarily wrong, but they are presented in the dream in a style of either/or opposition. If the dream-man insisted on having his way, the anima-girl would see him as an insensitive bully. He would see her as a painful presence, with her faintheartedness and disgusting hair. The potential for head-on collision of two views is all too evident. The clarity of the dream, however, makes possible a widening of consciousness to take account of both. This demands that the dreamer loosen his conscious attitudes enough to receive into awareness the textures of the anima component of his personality, on the one hand, and to disidentify himself from the charge-ahead momentum of the dream ego on the other hand. Such loosening may comprise a threatening expansion of boundaries to him, to say the least.

No less threatening is a man's attempt to see himself from the point of view of an important woman in his life. This effort allows him to make a feeling bridge to the female that may help him to receive her actual reality rather than seeing in her only what he needs or wants. In receiving her, he may discover how she receives him, which may in turn enlarge his view of himself.

In a relationship between lovers, this sort of knowing-through-identifying leads to a love well beyond the conventional. Too often only warm cooperation occurs between two separate selves, a kind of mutual respect and appreciation between parallel beings that never really come together. The alternate route, adding the less than conscious knowing-by-being-one-with, is a mingled love, no mere partnership of parallel beings. Here two become one flesh, gaining from each other the outward bodily possession of their inner contrasexual parts. A woman now possesses a phallus through the body of her lover—not a generalized organ, some kind of abstract spiritual potency, but the specific, concrete, personal phallus of her beloved. A man now has a concrete feminine organ of containment in the personal, specific vagina of his lover—not some spiritualized feminine receptivity in the abstract that is talked about more than lived, but an emblem in the flesh of what has happened to him in the spirit. In becoming one, always surprisingly, the two really gain twoness, each self enlarging as a result of the intermingling. Because this enlargement threatens our tight little self-image, we often fear the loss of ego boundaries in this mingling with a beloved. Many of us flee such possibilities of love, as a result.

In Christian religious experience this knowing-through-identifying refers to those mysterious moments often described as losing oneself for Christ's sake and finding oneself as a result. All religious experience—positive or negative—knows this process. We feel put into another dimension, whether of altered consciousness or consciousness raised; the boundaries of self and other no longer define a relationship but comprise a union. In this sort of experience we can well feel the loss of our human world altogether, and the possibility of being blown right off the map.

These fears point to real dangers. All these experiences characterized by the feminine way of knowing-through-identifying bring with them a kind of dissociating with what we consciously define as our selves. This sort of knowing accents receiving as against differentiating-from, extending our boundaries to include the other in contrast to mere self-preoccupation. Fearful though it may be, this feminine way of knowing, as Holbrook points out, is essential to such fundamental human experiences, as "dreams, phantasies, insights, telepathy, 'togetherness,' the electricity between lovers."[10] To these I would add the currents of emotion that make a group into a community, the ordinary mother's love of her baby, and the palpable experience of hope.

Flowing from this kind of knowledge through identification is the third feminine element, what we may call a sense of personal continuity. We experience our personal being rooted all the way back in the time of our birth and even before, and stretching forward into the future in an unbroken line of what Winnicott calls "going on being."[11] An unforced mode of doing in relation to the world issues from this continuous sense of self. Rooted deep in the unconscious origins of the psyche, a sense of being branches out to connect us in an organic way with both present and future.

We go all the way back to the time of our birth and before that, to being held in our mother's body, and even before that, to our spiritual conception in the love between our mother and father. Children love to hear stories of their birth; how it happened, and further, how they were planned for and awaited before their actual arrival. We glimpse here the psychological roots of the doctrine of the preexistence of Christ as the eternal Logos who was with God before the creation of the world. Being in this sense is a living continuity, which children somehow understand or want to understand. Our being moves forward into becoming, thus achieving its direction in the world. From such being-at-the-core and being-one-with and a sense of uninterrupted being grows the confidence to do, to make something out of our experience in a way that reflects awareness of other persons' being too. Our capacity to be endows us with a capacity to perceive and respectfully receive the being of others, and so forms the basis for any future ethical or moral allegiance we may adopt.

Many of us, however, cannot rely on such a sense of continuity. We do not feel we go all the way back into the hidden origins of existence. We lack a clear experience of being-at-the-core and as a result fear that in our being-one-with-another, which we so much desire, we may destroy the fragile sense of self we have barely managed to create. The sure establishment of self may have been interrupted by blows of fate—through the loss of a loving parent, perhaps, or through a neglectful or abusive parent, or crushing physical or mental illness, or a barren psychological environment, or the sudden failure of a love relationship. Lacking real being, we take refuge in what Guntrip so aptly calls "false-doing."[12]

False-doing takes various forms. We all know the meaningless activity, a sort of make-believe work without essential substance, that comes to substitute for real labor. We know the fruitless doing of an impersonal bureaucracy that simply replicates itself like a cancer, killing off healthy interaction between persons under onslaughts of memos, provisos, amendments, position papers. False-doing forces doing with no roots in being. False-doing manufactures a sense of being we do not possess. Religion used as illusion, crutch, or weapon, is false-doing. So is theology that no longer articulates our reception of God-with-us, but obsessively turns out proof systems or how-to political religions that assault us with formulas for social change as new idols to worship. False-doing, in place of a mother's willingness to be with her baby, substitutes doing things for the child—compulsive feeding schedules or a self-conscious lack of schedules that is just as demanding. False-doing is the war of the sexes—of the chauvinist male and the castrating female who appear to be so opposed to each other, but who in fact cooperate in their conspiracy to avoid feminine elements of being.

HATRED OF THE FEMALE

The war of the sexes expresses itself particularly in hatred of the female, which is hatred that arises from fear of the feminine elements of being: of being-at-the-core, of being-one-with, of the being that possesses personal continuity. Hatred of the female arises from hatred of the feminine elements of being in both sexes —of being human as being vulnerable, susceptible, with a sense of doing flowing from our sense of being.

A double displacement, first mentioned in Chapter 1, occurs, a displacement of attitude and content, from fear to hate and from generalized elements of being to particular female persons. We protect ourselves against this fear that makes us feel passive and helpless by changing it into an aggressive hate. We project these fearful elements onto women, trying to isolate them and control them by subjugation. Prejudice against women functions fundamentally as a massive defense against the fearful elements of being human that the feminine symbolizes.

One remarkable example is the way some existentialist philosophers and psychiatrists have contributed to hatred of the female. Lacan's theory of language associates basically hateful experiences to women. Lacan reasons this way: In relation to the mother, a child suffers a dual and devastating loss. First the child loses the immediacy of self, replacing it with a mirror image reflected in the mother's face. The child initially believes this imaginary unity with the mother to be the self's true image. The second loss is to discover the separate and different existence of the mother. The female is thus associated with lost unity within the self, a sort of shrinkage of the original larger self, and then with ruptured unity with this first and most important other, the precursor of all others. This lost and ruptured unity is associated in French existentialist thought with the inevitable alienation, emptiness, and void that Sartre, for example, claims is characteristic of the human condition. The British psychiatrist R. D. Laing asserts the inevitability of this condition when he insists we all live in dreadful alienation, destroyed at our mother's breasts by hate and disillusion.[13]

Lacan asserts that language fills this inevitable void and enables us to master its pain, a notion that promotes the dominance of discursive thought over other modes of mentation. From here, it is not far to jump to a prejudice against the female as a modern-day Eve introducing alienation (what the Bible calls sin) into the world, a rupture that only the male with his verbal intellect can fill.[14]

How different is Winnicott's view, to take but one contrary example, of the ordinary, good-enough mother who delights in her child's growing independence and encourages the pleasures of increased mutuality that accompany it. Here the female is just herself, with her own particular style of displaying the archetypal maternal theme in its positive mode, flowing with life and receiving its unfolding into its unique expressions in this particular child.

Perhaps Lacan and Laing and those like them spin their philoso-
phies out of a witch's cave, finding there those intensely negative
experiences of maternal failure. What they fail to note is their
substitution of a part for the whole, their abstract, globalized
projections of loss and alienation onto the female in place of facing
their own particular, and no doubt deep, pain of an often betrayed
and always betrayable vulnerability.[15]

We must all, men and women alike, admit to this vulnerability
in its most terrifying modes, but also see the graces it brings. For
we recover the being we lost, or never achieved in the first place,
when we return to the vulnerable state of being-with-another and
permit a continuous thread of being to develop through time
without denying it, displacing it onto women, resisting its pull, or
trying to snap it off altogether. Too often, however, we defend
instead, and, much more than we usually recognize, in terms of
attack on the being of others.

To defend against this threatening vulnerability—to others, to
the unconscious, to God—hatred is made into a false good in place
of love. Hatred is turned into a commercial commodity. Violence
is sold in myriad forms as a substitute way of feeling alive. As one
sixteen-year-old boy put it poignantly to his mother, "I don't feel
real unless I am in a dangerous situation."

From the fear of being vulnerable arises a lust for rigidly
defined political states. Dictatorships of attitude, doctrine, and
taste, such as those of Marxism, sexism, moralism, make us less
vulnerable because everything is laid out. We need no longer be
at one with others because all relations are defined in advance.
We need worry no more about concrete men and women because all that is a thing of the past, a bourgeois delusion. If we
defend against the inner core of our own being, inevitably we act
in society at the expense of the inner being of other persons. We
interrupt their being, whether with bullets or ideological tyran-
nies of the word from the point of view of the left or the right.

We will not consent that others be any more than we have ourselves consented to be.

False-doing arises from interruption of being. Instead of possessing a continuity of being from which a vigorous and unforced doing flows naturally, nurtured by mothers or lovers or God, we suffer a crumbling at the center of ourselves. Our being has been invaded, taken over by alien elements, and exists now only in fragments. We are not seen or reflected back to ourselves and thus no true self forms at the core.[16] Instead of finding our face reflected in the loving gaze of our mother, we see her preoccupied with her own problems and using us for their solution. The child is unnaturally forced to mother the mother. Instead of finding in religion affirmation for our human being in all its perplexity and possibility, moral prescriptions dictate how we should be, creating guilt in us for failing to measure up. Instead of forming a true self under the beneficent gaze of a loving other who reflects us back to ourselves, we assign ourselves, or are assigned, a role to play through the other's unconscious projections. We erect a warning system that will repel invasion and hide our vulnerable core behind an impenetrable wall. In thus protecting our dependent, unformed being, we seal its fate. It remains locked up and inaccessible behind a shell of defenses against being hurt. If we cannot be found, our reasoning goes, we cannot be hurt.

We soon come to fear being seen as much as not being seen. In this blind state we cannot see others either, except as prospective dangers to be warded off. Hence we contaminate others with our own failure to be. We fail to respect their being-at-the-core and have no capacity to be-one-with them or act toward them in a natural unforced way. Without recognition and nurturing of the being-at-the-core of all persons, our political arrangements to secure more justice come to nothing. Our hopelessness about "the system," whatever the system may be, stems from our hopelessness about ever being able to live as our true selves.

Worst of all, this fear of being grows into a hatred of being, summed up and symbolized in hatred of the female. The female as mother reminds us of our once absolute dependency and open vulnerability that we have now come to fear and from which we barricade ourselves behind all sorts of false-doing. Traditional symbolism associates to the feminine figure a being-one-with through identifying—a meditative gaze, a light touch, a sensitive hearing of what is said beneath the spoken words. This sort of knowing threatens to get behind our defenses and reveal us as we really are. We fear being susceptible, vulnerable, and open in this way. Hatred of the soul's capacity to be ravished by God is part of this great gathering into projections onto women—and is either firmly located there or repudiated through displacement onto a total rejection of the female sex. In the hatred of the female, expressed in projection, rejection, or whatever, lurks the hatred of being which we cannot drive away no matter how respectable we try to make it in the jargons of justice, politics, or the new sexuality. We can only deal with fear of being by turning directly to it and integrating it. For this we need the wisdom and modality of religion.

5

The Birth of Otherness:
The Feminine Elements of Being
and the Religious Life

When we receive into our consciousness these feminine elements of being, vulnerability, interdependence, and personal continuity, we learn how much they have to teach us about God's action in our lives. Instead of rejecting these elements, projecting them outward, and building defensive systems of hate and control, our life now takes an entirely different turn. Otherness is born in the midst of ordinary human affairs. The way of otherness is wide and long. To focus upon it, I have chosen to look at its beginnings, at the birth of religious experience and the spiritual life.

We can learn a great deal about spiritual and psychological birth from a woman's birth-giving experience in all its aspects—physical, psychological, spiritual—and from the early relationship between a mother and child. Essential to each experience is the perception of the other, not as an extension of myself, not as I would like that other to be, not as I may try to force the other to become, but as that other really is. To see the other with candor and appreciation for what objectively is there is a requisite for learning.

One's capacity to recognize the other begins, I think, with a mother's recognition of the otherness of her child. It involves the clear certainty that the child is a person different from herself, however intimately related to her. What happens in this first relationship is determinative for a child's whole life, helping to shape the capacity to see herself or himself as a person of individual value, not duplicated in anyone else. A secure grasp of the value of one's self makes it possible to see the value of other selves and of other beings. The recognition of otherness gives one a latitude and depth of relationship to the world, to culture, to other people, and eventually to one's own children.

There can be no religious or psychological experience of consequence without recognition of otherness. Experiences may exhilarate us, shake us, or arouse us to new insights, but these are not religious or psychological events of consequence unless they contain an unmistakable presence of something other than ourselves. This other announces itself as something related to us, but so different from us that we cannot see it as part of our own selves. Even if absorbed by an ecstatic vision, after it fades we recognize that what was present was not ourselves or any part of ourselves.

The mother-child relationship and religious experience are both inward and personal. In both kinds of experience one discovers areas of human life where barely understood forces or presences are at work. One may respond psychologically and with a sense of religious awe to the intimation of value present at such depth. The notion of worth at this level of being forms one's day-to-day consciousness. Such depth experience shapes our goals and desires; it contains qualities on which one depends; it possesses value in the sense of setting standards that measure the extent of one's surrender to it. Both the mother-child relationship and religious experience nurture this deep-rooted value that is born in the recognition of otherness.

TWO DIRECTIONS OF VALUE

A mother-child relationship and a religious experience indicate two directions in which the conferring of value may take place: from the self to the other and from the other to the self. Clearly a mother's recognition of her child as a distinct person communicates a sense of value to the child. Also God's addressing us in word, vision, or historical act confers upon us a moving sense of the divine as a primary source of value, and of our own worth as recipients of value. Less obvious in each case is the conferring of value in the other direction. The mother is given a new sense of her own value by recognizing the otherness of her child, and a person's response to God's presence confers value upon that experience. In each relationship the conferring of value is reciprocal—from the self to the other and the other to the self.

In the mother-child relationship, the child gains initial recognition of otherness from being seen as someone quite other than the parent; but so does the mother. Her identity is changed because she is seen as other than what she thinks herself. She then perceives something other in herself than she did before. If she really recognizes this new other she is becoming, the experience will take on a larger dimension and change her entire life.

An illustration of this idea occurred when a middle-aged woman sought analysis because of a recurring problem of low self-esteem. In our first interview she told how her son as a little boy had stirred her to claim herself as a person of value. At that time she weighed over two hundred pounds, dressed poorly, and let her husband make every kind of decision. She felt she had no thought, no initiative, no feeling to contribute to anything. The redeeming events in her life were the coming of her children, a girl and a boy. She felt their births and subsequent presence in her life were nothing short of miraculous. One day when she picked up her son from kindergarten, he said to her that his teacher was the "second ugliest woman in the world." The unspoken question of who was the first hung in the air until she could no longer bear it, and so she asked him who was the ugliest. "You are, Mommy," he replied, "the first ugliest woman in the world." Shocked by her son's frank description of her, she saw herself with a terrible clarity she had heretofore suppressed. This conversation set off a revolution within her; she began to take herself seriously indeed. She lost weight, learned to dress with flair, and eventually became an office manager for a business firm. Even now, twenty years later, she knows she would never have sought help without her son's blunt perception of what she looked like. This child, whom she had nurtured and now beheld as a wondrous other, in turn nurtured in her a new sense of self-value.

In an analogous way, God's recognition of us confers value from the divine to the human. Equally, our response to the revelatory events of Scripture contributes to their value. By receiving God's love we participate in it, nurturing those moments that have nurtured us, adding our own sense of value to the inestimable value given in the mystery of our being. Thus we contribute to the sense of value given to us by giving love back to its source. Our nurturing response nurtures the nurturer. Why else would Yahweh mourn the defection of Israel, or Jesus weep for those who turn away from him?

Recognizing the other, then, is instinct with a sense of value, whether it is the value of oneself, of another person, or of life itself. Further, I would insist that the events that mark the initial relation between mother and child—conception, birth, and early development—also mark crucial moments in religious experience. Just as a mother's first attitudes to her child go a long way toward shaping the child's life, so in religious experience we are both child and mother. We nurture and protect the small beginnings of the spirit within us; yet we feel like fledglings watched over by the hovering spirit of the Lord. A mother's conscious and unconscious attitudes to these events are paradigmatic for all human responses to the early phases of religious experience.

Unfortunately, the dynamics of the earliest phases of human and religious life do not easily lend themselves to discussion because so much occurs at a preconscious level. To thread a way through this obscure territory, I propose first to discuss the concept of otherness and then its appearance in a mother's attitudes to the conception, birth, and early development of her child. I will also explore analogies between the mother-child relationship and religious experience.

THE CONCEPT OF OTHERNESS

The recognition of otherness depends on a number of convictions: the certainty of the presence of someone or something both different from and the same as ourself. In those moments when we recognize great likeness and great difference, we increase enormously our understanding of ourself and of the other. Otherness is a psychological-religious concept. Psychologically we must have a sense of the other in order to have a sense of self. Perception of otherness is indispensable for differentiation of the ego from the unconscious, of interior experience from outer reality, of a sense of our own personal identity from another person's reality. At the very minimum, the recognition of otherness defines where the "I" ends and the "other" begins. At a higher level, perception of the other affords the possibility of relationship as opposed to unconscious fusion of one person with another.

In its religious dimension otherness stands for the "not-me," what Harry Stack Sullivan calls a major component of any religious experience, as it makes itself felt in a sense of the dreadful uncanny. C. G. Jung says the other represents a "non-ego" which nonetheless intimately connects itself with ego consciousness.

Jung's name for this other is the "self." Through it what Jung calls the nonpersonal, "objective" psyche makes known to the ego its demand for relationship. Martin Buber builds most of his theology on a sense of otherness. The other is the famous "Thou" to whom the subject "I" must relate. Karl Barth sees the other as the Christ in whose depths man finds his true image reflected. Only through the other, through Christ, does man come to self-knowledge. Only by looking at Christ does man know himself both as sinner and as forgiven. For H. Richard Niebuhr, Christ lays bare the root metaphor of a Christian's inner personal history, symbolizing his identity and his connection to the world. Kierkegaard explores the religious significance of otherness most thoroughly by using it to distinguish the characteristics of the highest phase of spiritual development in his category of "Religiousness B." In "Religiousness A" we are related to God as the other, but we focus on our *own* experience of the other and on our *own* transformation in relation to the other, on our *own* eternal happiness rather than on the subject of eternal happiness. In "Religiousness B" we focus on the other, God as God's self, not on our experience of God.

What Kierkegaard describes as two separate stages helps to unmask a confusion that invades our understanding on the psychological level of the mother-child relationship.[1] A mother may fail to recognize the otherness of her child and see it really as an extension of herself. Caught up in *her* experience of the child, she is concerned with what the child makes her feel (as in "Religiousness A"), rather than being struck by what the child feels, by what the child experiences apart from her.

CONCEPTION

Psychoanalytical theorists describe the first months of relationship between an infant and its mother as symbiotic.[2] In symbiosis, there is little or no differentiation between mother and child. They live in psychological unity. The mother feels the child as part of herself.

On the basis of symbiosis between mother and child, analogies are drawn to a primary religious experience. We long to return to a symbiotic unity with God, to be safely held within the greatest possible power of being. We yearn for security and dependency, entirely supported by God's love. We seek containment within a mystery that will enfold our transiency within eternity. We want to be grounded in Being, just as an infant is joined to its mother's being. From this perspective, any move toward independence, any move away from symbiotic unity, is imbued with sadness. To be oneself is to be desolate, to be ejected from life's center.

In contrast to the theory of symbiosis, I am proposing a view based on my own experience and that of some of my patients. I would stress that even in a child's prenatal life, a mother may recognize otherness. Symbiosis is not necessarily predominant. A parent may be struck more by the discrete quality of her child's being than by its dependency on her. A child's otherness takes root in a conception that is spiritual before it is physical; it grows from the parents and their conception of each other's otherness. It is all bound up with how much the man and woman perceive the distinct being of each other, how much they receive of each other's uniqueness. For inevitably, parents conceive their child in the spirit of their relation to each other.

How do a couple envision having a child? What does it mean to them to do so, consciously and unconsciously? The child's earliest life reflects to a large degree its parents' conception of its presence. It is so easy to think of all the wrong reasons for having a child—as therapy for a sick marriage, as medicine for bruised self-esteem, as proof of sexuality. A child can too easily be used as a filler for an empty life, as meaning-giver for a lost soul. One of the rarest of all human ventures is, on the contrary, to conceive a child as free, as a gift given with no prescribed role attached.

Together child and parents then build a new range of identities as they construct their relationship. Conceived in this spirit, a child evokes a love of Being, simply because Being, like the new child, is alive and there.

When physical conception occurs in this positive way, a spiritual conception of otherness develops quickly. The initiation of human life introduces into relationship an extraordinary plane of value. The parents now sense the beginnings of a person and of the process by which human value is brought into the world.

Parents contribute greatly to a child's experience of itself at birth, just by their attitude toward its coming. If parents nourish the value of a child, just as a mother's body nourishes the embryo, a child will gather value all during pregnancy. This strongly influences the will of that child to live, and to live with value. There is no psychological gain for the child if even before it is born it is seen merely as an extension of its parents. The "sense of person" of this new person is downgraded from the start. This failure to esteem the other, even in one's own child, reflects a low esteem of one's own person.

Women who have been through difficult birth experiences say that the value nourishment given the child throughout pregnancy has strongly influenced their child's will to live at birth. From the first, the child seems to have radiated a sense of its own value. A distinct other has appeared who was not before and who could so easily not have been. Its appearance seems to draw upon all the months of dark nourishment in the womb and all that in the semiconsciousness of the parents told them that this new life was other than their own.

When emphasis is placed on recognizing a child's otherness, even in its prenatal state, the father's role takes on a new significance, too. He is no longer out of things because he is not carrying the child. Nor is he confined merely to supporting the mother, bringing some sort of encouragement before, during, and after the child's birth, vitally important as that kind of support may be. His important contribution lies in his own recognition of his child's otherness all through the gestation period. He also begins to orient himself in relation to this new other who is already present and yet is still to be. He helps construct a setting in which to house the growing child just as his wife's body expands to provide it physical space. In such ways the unity of parents' love may reflect the child's otherness.

The Denial of Otherness

Parents can easily miss seeing the otherness of their child and make everybody suffer as a result. The denial of otherness usually occurs in two ways. In the first, a mother consciously sees her offspring as an extension of herself, but unconsciously experiences her child as too much of an other—as a threat. The otherness that is suppressed from consciousness appears in the unconscious in exaggerated form. The child now seems to menace the mother's own identity. The conflict a woman patient suffered with both her son and daughter illustrate this clearly. The mother was thirty-three, her daughter was six, her son three. She sought therapeutic help because of irrational outbursts of hatred toward her children. When they were infants she had not felt this hatred. As they grew older she found herself exploding in anger—anger out of all proportion to the incidents—and filling with resentment at their very presence. After several months of therapy, a complicated conflict came to light as the cause of her hatred of the children. This woman had long been living in a state of unconscious identity with her own mother. She felt herself still, in her adult life, to be essentially an extension of her mother's existence. Her feelings about her own mother, her sense of oneness with that parent, were the most important feelings she had about anyone. To acknowledge that her own children were not just extensions of herself, but beings other than herself, severely disrupted her sense of her own identity as a comfortable and unchallenging extension of her mother. Throughout pregnancy, birth, and the infant years of both children's lives, she continued the suppression of their otherness by treating them as her property, to be governed as she saw fit. This proprietary attitude set up rebellious responses in her offspring. She often felt that each child preferred whatever was opposite from herself. The otherness of the children that she was thus forced to accept made her recognize the value of her own otherness as a person.

In extreme cases, a woman's sudden shift in awareness from seeing her child as simply an extension of herself to seeing it as other than herself can produce a dissociation of psychotic proportions. As long as such a woman carries the unborn baby within her, the baby is felt not only as a part of her body but as the best part. The baby's presence gives her identity: as a pregnant woman, entitled to courtesy, consideration, and curious glances, she receives from others many happy projections of maternal bliss. More important still, the baby within her guarantees in a visible way that she is not empty or without significance. On the contrary, she knows she is filled up with a life that testifies to her inner substance and her power to create something out of herself.

The second principal way of denying a child's otherness is just the opposite of this first case. In the example that follows, the mother consciously regarded her son as an other existing in his own right, but unconsciously identified with him as exclusively an extension of her own personality.

This is the case of a woman of thirty-nine who had two sons (aged ten and eight) when unexpectedly she became pregnant again. From birth, her third child suffered severe constipation that turned out to be medically untreatable. In other areas of his life this little boy was normal. He was a charming person, articulate and original. He got along well with other children and adults. He seemed to understand more about his own bowel problem than anyone else. When five years old, he said: "Just wait, Mommy. When I am older, I will be well."

The boy's difficulty did not fully clear up until his mother finally dealt with her feelings about him in analysis. On the conscious level the mother was very fond of her son and had an excellent relation to him. She enjoyed him, liked and even admired him. Unconsciously, however, she thought of him as strictly hers, as an unmistakable extension of her own secret life. With great difficulty, she revealed that for years she had indulged in random sexual relations for money, gifts, canceled debts. At the time she became pregnant this behavior still occasionally occurred. The beginnings of this child were symbolically bound up with this heavy secret.

She explained her earlier behavior as necessary. Her husband was addicted to alcohol and took all their money to support his drinking bouts. They lived on the edge of financial disaster. By occasional prostitution, she was able to feed and clothe her children and herself and keep their apartment. She still loved her husband and did not want to divorce him.

I raised the possibility that her concealing of this secret life of hers, with its accompanying guilt, was being expressed physically in her child's constipation. I asked her if she could tell her husband these things. She said no, it was out of the question. Curiously, however, confessing these things coincided with the first lessening of her son's symptoms. She thought about telling her husband everything and of sharing an open life with him. She also became aware of how much she had shielded her son from her husband. Her unconscious assumption that the boy was "hers" found expression in her confinement of the child to herself. As her behavior changed, her youngest son and her husband developed a closer relationship.

At this point the woman discontinued treatment. Not until several years later, after the husband had sought treatment for his alcoholism, did the wife share more of her past life with her husband. She came to see me again at this time. She told me that when she told her husband what she had kept secret, she felt a tremendous sense of letting go, of coming out into the open, a freedom to be herself and to face her husband's anger and hurt and forgiveness, and finally to accept herself. The child was cured, almost miraculously. His constipation simply went away. He was free now to let go and to be himself, no longer having to carry his mother's unconscious burdens. He could be someone other than his mother.

Although this is an extreme example, the general effect of greeting otherness is to open for inspection the deep, dark secrets of one's life which one has not had the courage to face before.

CONCEPTION AND RELIGIOUS EXPERIENCE

If a woman does not consciously or unconsciously ignore the otherness of the child growing within her, how does she regard it? What have such responses to do with the cultivation of religious experience? After conception, a woman turns inward. She is tired, less conscious, pulled downward, as if to be free to revolve around a new focus. A pregnant woman weaves half-conscious fantasies about herself in relation to her baby, fantasies scarcely capable of verbalization. She is preoccupied because she is thoroughly occupied; she becomes a residence for an other, and responds to *its* presence with a sense of *its* value. She feels linked to it, yet altogether different from it, housing it, holding it, creating an inner space for it and being created anew herself as this other accommodates itself to her.

Similarly, the nascent stages of religious experience are conceived in darkness. Often we do not know what began the process or when. We only know something has happened that initiates a long process of coming to terms with the otherness of the spirit. A mother's attitudes toward physical conception suggest many ways of nourishing this small beginning of an active response to mystery. Instead of trying to relate to the first implantation of religious life directly and with intellectual understanding, like a new mother we circle around it. We allow it to fill our attention and become a new focal point for gathering and nurturing rich and enlarging wishes.

Wishes contain desires and desires motivate actions. By giving play to our wishes for religious experience, for relation to mystery, for a spiritual life, we allow our desires time to ripen into intentions. Intentions are necessary to sustain action so that gradually we may be rescued from an undirected impulsiveness that only leaves us exhausted. Slowly we build up stamina to persist in the long process of acquiring relationship with this "other" of the spirit, much as a woman's body gradually expands to house a new person. Wishing thus grows into hope, hope for the capacity to commit ourselves to the desired coming of the spirit. Wishes are the essential ingredient, the instinct power of hope.

Many people who complain of the paucity of religious life suffer from loss of hope. They have lost hope because they have forgotten how to wish. The power of wishing persists just below the surface of our minds. Wishes are attached to instincts that press for release as long as we are fully alive. To begin to recover the power of hope, we must sink into our wishes and dare to claim them. Like the figure of Mary pondering in her heart the words of annunciation, we must meditate upon this other of the spirit who has penetrated us. But to ponder and meditate is to suspend judgment and to allow the play of fantasy. We try varied ways of relating to the spirit, yet wait for it to show itself in its own time and place. Our fantasies draw on the power of our wishes; they bind us to the other in an attitude of intense participation.

Slowly, under these circumstances, fantasy develops into imagination, which in turn actively responds to its inner spiritual content. Much as a mother imagines the ways in which she will react to her newborn child, the person implanted with a new religious life imagines the shape it will take and what change it will produce. The drifting and dreaming quality of fantasy becomes focused in our imagination on how we will relate to the "other." Our own identity begins to change imperceptibly. The "I" slowly transforms into a "we." Self can only be known through its connection to this indwelling other. The strange psychological and physical metamorphosis a pregnant woman undergoes is a model for all spiritual transformation. We are no longer just ourself; we are also the other. Yet we stand separate from the other, intimately linked but not identified with it.

Imagination captures the transformation of the spirit. From simple images of particular experiences of the spirit grow the large symbols and visions of religious tradition. We lose connectedness with tradition and doctrine when we lose touch with even subliminal images in our experience of mystery. Dogma seems dry, outmoded, sterile when we have no point of contact with the hidden vitality of the spirit. However, the wide reaches of religious mystery and symbol—the stages of Mass, Communion, and related worship; the stages of Christ's way to the cross; the visions of the New Jerusalem—come to us through those primitive images that express the deep meaning of our own experience of mystery at no matter how prosaic a level. To feel the lifeblood that flows through religious imagery we must find the pulse of our own daily experience of life. Just as a mother cannot imagine what life is like from her child's point of view if she neglects what life is like for herself in relation to that child, so the novice in the spiritual life must nurture every tiny experience through imaginative responses to it. Only then do we find a bridge to the record that religious tradition has made of human experience of the divine.

What stands out in both physical and spiritual conception is a quality of particularity. A mother slowly centers around a particular human life growing within her. Mothers of several children report that each baby announces itself in its own way in the womb, kicking, turning, or remaining quiet. Similarly, each segment of religious experience has its own distinct presence. Each one gradually centers around a particular content that achieves its own shape in its own time, demanding sustained participation from its "host." This particularity of focus gradually intensifies into an act of concentration; we not only center around the other, we are centered by its presence in the midst of our being. To grow in concentration means not only to become less distracted; it means to be purified. The essential experience is distilled into an unadulterated form, with all else discarded.

We have much to learn from a woman's attitudes in the gestation period. Wishing, fantasy, imagination, and concentration preside together over this process. We learn in the course of it that wishing empowers hope, and fantasy produces acts of imagination that create from particular moments extraordinary visions that extend from the human to the divine.

Just as a woman may deny the otherness of her children, so we may try to deny the otherness of the spirit and with the same disastrous results. We may try to "have" a religious experience to bolster our faltering sense of self. We may claim the stirrings of the spirit within us as extensions of our own egos, something we alone have produced. This will only result in our estrangement from that other, who, like a child finding no room in our hearts for its special presence, will leave us. We may fear the otherness of the spirit and repress our awareness of it. This can only lead to crippling burdens of undelivered feelings, and even to guilt.

BIRTH

No matter how intimately a woman makes her being one with the baby growing within her, the baby shapes her life even more than she does herself. She cannot control who this other will be

—what sex, what state of health, what kind of personality. All these must be announced to her along with the baby's first cry at birth. At this moment not only a child is born but also a mother; a woman begins a new life with a new identity along with her child. In some cases a woman's identity changes radically as a result of giving birth. One case, that of a reserved, withdrawn, and frightened woman, afflicted with a bad case of stuttering, communicates this very well. She used a logical, reasoning approach to life to protect herself from any rush of emotion. Everything, she believed, must proceed according to standards of justice and of right and wrong. Strong emotion threatened her; it often left her defenseless, prey to fears, out of control. When this woman gave birth to a daughter she also gave birth to her own capacity to feel. For example, she wrote her husband her first love letter, full of passionate gratitude for his help during her labor. She gave way for the first time to a deep need to depend upon him, and to the inexpressible love that her dependency carried with it. With her daughter, she enjoyed a whole new range of feeling. She sang to her baby, called her love-names, kissed her, played with her endlessly. In word and gesture, she allowed herself free rein to demonstrate her feelings.

Birth is an act as well as an event. A woman's participation is required, yet it is a paradoxical participation. She actively brings forth new life from herself yet receptively attunes herself to this emerging other in order to follow its lead. Even artificial inducement of labor must be adjusted to indications from the baby that it is ready to come forth.

Whenever a birth occurs, it is a decisive event for both mother and child. It is an event that lends itself to the creation of an oral tradition that begins as soon as the mother tells her story of how her child came into the world. Maternity wards are full of such stories, told and retold many times. In such tellings every mother hears variations on the theme of her own experience of the mysterious event of being emerging out of nothing, of a human person culminating a long, dark interior process foreign to mind and to reason. Women gather around a new mother and child to trade accounts of their version of this mystery. Each remembers how it was for her with her own baby, sensing beneath the words the inexplicable depth of such experience. Often a mother tells her child these stories, sometimes even before the child can understand the words. Thus she introduces the child to the mystery of his or her own introduction to life. Such a story can be negative in its telling as well as warmly positive. A mother may complain that she never had such pain as this child gave her. She may report that she wept when she first saw the child, wishing it were the other sex. She may imply that the birth experience was so bad she could never want to have children again. Positive or negative, the telling of the birth story underlines receiving the mystery of otherness. In the most ordinary event mystery announces itself in a happening that recurs countless times. In a process explained biologically and rationally, the altogether wondrous has broken through.

Often women cannot believe they have brought forth something so good, so miraculous as a child. The first reaction of many a woman when her infant is first brought to her hospital room, all neatly wrapped, is to unwrap it and look at it hard. Even with the baby before her eyes, a woman finds it difficult to believe in the perfection of its form—its small toes and fingers, its smooth skin, its network of wrinkles and folds. She gazes at her child and meditates over its being. She receives it. Such a contemplative response often turns out to be the only way a woman can consciously absorb the impact of the mystery of birth, where otherness is truly born in the flesh. Her only alternative to living with mystery is to hide from it, repressing its presence and forgetting her participation in it when her child was born. If a woman takes this alternative, she usually experiences her child's otherness negatively.

BIRTH AND RELIGIOUS EXPERIENCE

Many parallels can be drawn between a mother's attitudes toward the birth of her child and the soul's attitudes toward spiritual birth. First of all, like a mother, a soul must wait for the right time. To push ahead impatiently only creates what might be called spiritual cramps; then one brings forth a premature product that has difficulty sustaining life. But to lag too far behind is to damage the content, bruising its form and perhaps even crippling its power irremediably. The soul must attune itself to the inner other of the spirit and follow its transforming lead. The soul both participates vigorously in the birth act and submissively receives the will and tempo of the "other" as it is brought into the world of personal actions and reactions. The time of this delivery, moreover, whether it be a physical or a spiritual birth, carries decisive authority. It is time as *kairos*. From its date all other times are reckoned as "before" or "after." New life has begun. This moment invests all other moments with value. A concrete and particular "other" has come into being. History is now possible.

This "other" of the spirit singles itself out as distinctly as a child does; it is concrete and particular, unique in its world as one child is unique among all other children. Such spiritual events take many forms. The spirit reaches us through a phrase in a book, arresting our attention, directing us to a new approach. Shrunken into silent despair, we may suddenly sense that the Lord sits there with us. The divine may strike us with a dazzling vision, leaving us limp and gasping. The spirit may pull us so that without thought we dumbly turn to the divine in all things as we blunder through a day. We sometimes hear the Lord's words when we hear another person's tumbling thoughts click into place and feel our connection with them.

Moving through all these different events is the mystery of an otherness that changes us whenever and wherever we meet it. Like a child living in its mother or like a mother surrounding a child, the soul carries its love of God and is enlarged by it. Such interpenetration of the human and the divine yields a comprehension that gathers up the total person. Such knowledge is concrete, not abstract, particular, not general; it cannot be imparted or proved. Like a woman in childbirth, the reality of such a comprehensive experience can scarcely be put into words, let alone generally applied. Such an experience is conditioned by the personality that carries it off; it cannot be de-emotionalized or translated into isolated bits of general information. The soul can only tell its own story; its authority consists in its particularity.

And the particular story must be told. It looms out of us, reaching into other people, even without anyone knowing what has happened. The story of our meeting with the divine mystery slips into our words without permission, plants its seeds without consent. It cannot be contained. It flashes forth to the world. We are carried along with the good news, flushed and excited in a swift eagerness to tell all, however little we may reveal of the large presence of the spirit. Even when we feast within ourself on the dark core of mystery, not wanting to share a morsel with anyone else, the great presence exudes a fragrance that others cannot miss, however inaccurately they may identify it. We have been changed, and people will ask what has happened. Like the good news of the gospel, our meeting with mystery creates its own space within our life, pressing to be shared with others. Just as women flock to see a new baby and hear of its arrival, each wanting to hold the child, to touch it, to marvel over it as if to peer into the very face of mystery, so people unconsciously are pulled toward the presence of the spirit. Like the mother with her birth story, each small development in the bringing forth of spiritual life evolves its own oral tradition. Such meetings with the divine demand an image-laden vocabulary of stories, parables, and gestures. The spirit flies forth like a wild bird and our words run after it, not to miss any of its flight.

Our response to religious experience is like a woman's response at childbirth when she is astonished that something so good could have come from her. Often she feels a mixture of horror and wonder as she looks at the red splotches of her baby's skin and feels its wailings pitched at her in unnerving sound. She grabs at any reassurance that her baby is normal; she finds security in statistics that show that her reactions are normal too. Similarly we always marvel that some sense of the divine did grow in us. The spirit planted a seed in us, of all people, and it took root. Those who bring forth a sense of God's otherness always need assurance—that what has come to them is good and true and that they themselves are sane and safe and well.

Early Development

In the first months of a baby's life, a mother and child must get to know each other, to receive each other and establish what Erikson has called basic trust.[3] A baby needs to know that someone is there who is reliable, friendly, and responsive. A baby also needs to know that he or she is reliably there as a self, worthy of trust and capable of friendliness and responsiveness. Mother and child act and react in mutuality as a working unit, as what D. W. Winnicott calls a "nursing couple."[4]

To achieve mutuality it is essential to receive otherness. A mother sees right away that her child is other than herself and different from previous children she may have had. A new child punctuates her day in a new way, in its own style, setting its own standards for eating, sleeping, and walking. A child perfects its own fuss-quotient and hangs on to and gives up its mother's breast, or the bottle, when the time is right.

A mother discovers that she too is different from the person she used to be. Her range of hearing develops acuity, alert even through sleep to catch one particular voice tossed up from the depths of the crib. Yet she can drop into deep sleep anytime, anywhere. Her endurance toughens; she pushes through a day even when exhausted.

The otherness of her child demands a response from her. Her response may be positive or negative. She may receive the distinct being of her child, or she may reject it. She may shrink from the pleasure her baby releases, fearing its abundance. Her delight in beholding her child's little face, its curled hand, its frowsy, downy head, its greedy mouth, may all but suffocate her. She may feel overwhelmed by having had a baby at all and cling to rules and regulations as a way of guarding herself from the impact of its presence. Structure may spell safety to her, keeping her from losing herself to all these many emotions that are sweeping through her. She may even fear this other that is so distinctly itself, and feel the baby is judging her, weighing her, and finding her wanting.[5] Stunned that this other ever came into life, a new mother may fear she cannot sustain it. Relentlessly she will joggle and fondle her baby, sing to it to get a smile, a giggle, a noise, anything to reassure her that her baby is fully alive. Stubbornly, such a mother supervises every new experience in every possible detail in order to quell her nervousness so that nothing will go wrong.

It is the wonder of being that is so hard to receive. Most mothers never fully accept the fact that a baby has been born to them and is really alive. Crammed into the most ordinary routine of nursing, changing, bathing, playing with her child is the miracle of being, the mystery of the person, the extraordinary fact of otherness.

To look hard at this mystery may often be the best way a woman can find to live with it. A mother returns to the nursery repeatedly to look at her child sleeping, to watch it breathing, to gaze at its face, its feet, at every movement of its body. She takes it in; she allows its otherness to penetrate her; she gives it her attention. This particular way of looking shuns sentimentality; she sees the child as the child is, not as she wishes or needs the child to be. Its way of announcing desires, its gestures and tonalities, its dim sense of otherness as its wide-eyed staring takes her in—all pierce her consciousness. As the child increasingly recognizes her, her attention transforms into presence; two beings mutually present themselves to each other. Out of this special attention communication gradually evolves. Mothers learn to speak the special vocabulary of their infants and act as their translators.

As a mother and her infant establish basic trust between them, so the novice in spiritual life seeks ways of trusting the other that is just beginning to make itself known. The novice must gain assurance that that other is reliably there, possessed of objective existence, and is not simply an illusion produced by wishful thinking, imperious needs, or a dubious pathology. One must gradually submit to faith so that the other will show responsive concern and give one the strength to withstand its presence.

As a mother's responsibilities are stretched, changed, and sharpened by a child, so we are changed by the sense of otherness that touches us in religious experience. Through hard, tough, and courageous looking at this other our capacity to receive other people is expanded, transformed, and made acute. Centered by this meeting with otherness, all our meetings with people, things, ideas, facts, and places are now interleaved with a double sense of self and other. We blur less and submit more. We are less rigid and more firm. We drift less because we hold more to clear marks. We hoard less because we treasure more. We cheat less because we give more away.

The pleasure aroused in a mother by her child also has its exact parallels in religious experience. Whatever the form through which one is touched by otherness, it is always in the body; the experience is deeply fixed in our flesh. We may fear this and cancel it out by reducing it to sexual hallucinations, much as many modern psychologists try to reduce saints' visions to sexual frustration. We may try to disembody our experience of God, to reduce it to an idea or a psychic insight because we fear the sexuality in it. We may hedge the pleasure we feel so strongly with rules and regulations to stifle its growth. We may want constant assurance that such an experience really did happen and really is good. Thus we are forever joggling, tweaking, holding, and turning our experience of the other like a mother prodding her child to get it to smile, constantly trying to produce new and reassuring signs of life.

If we can receive the pleasure of this new presence in us with ease, the pleasure may develop in us a great and enlarging sense of play. Wishes can be given rein and fantasy allowed to mature into imagination. Images expressive of our spiritual encounters may lead us deeper into ourselves and into the world; we can come in and go out of ourselves with ease and freshness. Less dependent on the mold of the moment for our earnestness, we may now more fully consent to the ways of prayer playing through us. Pleasure will save us from trying too hard and thus relying too much on our own efforts. We can submit to the constant play of the Lord's efforts to reach us with the riches of mystery. When we receive the pleasure of God's presence, we realize its concreteness. The other of the spirit makes itself known through the material of our life, our character, images, needs, gropings, loves, and hates. The spirit resides within us, housed by our psychological being, feeding on it, circulating in our blood, brought forth in our adaptation to the world, changing that world, our relationships, and our mental being. Its presence grows within, as a child grows within its mother, and is bodied forth into the world as a child is born. We feel personally related to this other as a mother does to her infant. Our relationship to it is composed of touching and being touched; it is intimate, not abstract; the spirit is near, not remote.

The spirit lives within us, changes us, comes forth out of the stuff of our existence, yet in no way can we reduce it to a mere product of ourselves, a projection of our own invention. We are made by it, even as it takes shape within our lives. We have been penetrated by this other of the spirit; the random facts of our lives have been gathered up into intentionality. The divine has become historical; now we can at least dimly see our story pieced together with purpose, a story moving us all the more as we see it in relation to God's story shown in Christ.

Because the spirit steps toward us in the events of any ordinary day, religion is not different from everyday life, but is only its intensification and deepening. The most common event invokes the extraordinary. Just as each day is a miracle to each of the millions of women who have babies, so the spirit ignites the daily stuff of our lives no matter how prosaic or familiar. The great secret of Christian revelation is its availability. People hunt for the unusual, the far out, the obscure, the scorching vision, while the revelation seeks us exactly where we are.

To respond to the stirrings of the spirit within we need to be attentive to everything that is, to what comes to us at any moment. When a mother nags at her child to make it conform to her image of its personality, she misses the otherness proper to the child's own existence and her own uniqueness as well. When we twist our religious experience to match our preconceptions or sentimental notions, we only thrust away the other who is there. Only by receiving the being that is there can we develop trust and relationship. We neither identify with it nor detach ourselves from it but like a woman with her child accept its presence fully into our consciousness and respond to it fully.

This kind of attention brings with it a new kind of consciousness, not self-consciousness, but consciousness of the self, the self in relation to the other. We do not focus on *our* experience of the other but on the *other* and thus receive the self as well. In its highest form this kind of attention becomes contemplation, a dwelling upon the other that stirs deep changes of being. One exposes oneself to the mystery of otherness, not to remove it, but to receive it. One opens to the unknown in trust. Giving attention is transformed into giving oneself. Seeing the other becomes a contemplation of the other which transfigures the other into a revealing presence. We know God now as the elemental presence rooted in our own flesh, as born within us, in our own persons. In giving birth to religious experience we are reborn, resurrected into the world of presence, given over into abundant life where the other grants us ourselves.

6
The Authority of Women

Women today must face the issue of their own authority. We live in explosive times when traditional models for women no longer hold. Many women eschew motherhood; their journey into a spiritual life moves along quite different paths from those we considered in the last chapter. New models are insistently foisted upon us from every side. The bewildering variety threatens us. We are told that we must recognize ourselves as androgynous, or that a lesbian life really is a valid life-style, or that we must not be duped by any of these new ideas but implant old-fashioned motherhood in ourselves. Or we must strike out for a career lest we fail to be our own person. Every possible vision of the female is offered as a credible option, leaving us with the intoxicating freedom to find out own ways to be women, putting together as best we can a personal combination of background, tradition, innovation, and original experience to create a personal identity that will hold authority for us.

Such freedom is as arduous as it is liberating. The opportunities for personal definition are greater now than ever before precisely because of the loosening of conventional opinions, inherited values, religious convictions, political certainties, and social stereotypes. But without clearly articulated definitions to rebel against, complain about, and react to, the burden of creation presents, as Kierkegaard said, a dizzying effect. Our need for authority grows all the more urgent with every failure of nostrums and panaceas for quick and easy use. The locus of authority now shifts for women. They must recognize themselves as no mere variations on the male. The symbolism of the feminine is more than a complementary part of masculine images, and both stand for a special way of being and becoming, each with its own impetus and direction. Such an approach may lead to the discovery of an abiding authority that issues from women's own experiences.

Authority yields an extraordinary range of meanings. In Latin alone, it has these associations: to increase, to enlarge, to augment, to originate, to found, to author. Thus, in this understanding, one with authority can delegate power, adjudicate issues, possess persuasive force or conviction. In Greek, authority has a similar range of associations: to begin, beget, project, or stand forth with power, prominence, and dignity. More striking meanings come from the Hebrew: the one with authority is a maker, creator, nourisher, bestower, master, teacher, supreme counselor, one who carries a burden—the weight of dignity.[1]

To find our own authority as women we must look into our experience of the unconscious as well as what we know consciously, and out of those depths we must beget actions, engender persuasive force, nourish, counsel, conceive and develop distinct feminine perspectives from which to view reality. Jung's notion of the animus proves a useful metaphor that helps us come to terms with our own capacities to function in ways that have traditionally been assigned to men. To find our authority as women means we must integrate the animus—the so-called masculine side of ourselves—with our identities as females so that it is at our conscious disposal for use in our lives and in the world.

Jung's notion of the whole person as contrasexual is a radical twentieth-century image. It steers us clear of sex-role stereotypes where we must be exclusively male or female, pressured from within and without to squeeze ourselves to fit some abstraction called the feminine or the masculine, or take the consequences of guilt and ostracism if we fail to conform. Contrasexuality squarely faces the fact of concrete sexual identity. We are born into male or female bodies which shape our psychological perceptions of self and world. A parent of the same sex initiates different psychological dynamics in our development from those that come from a relationship with a parent of the opposite sex. Our sexual identity as men or women comprises a central part of our personality and cannot simply be ignored. It must be lived by us in a personal way, neither lacquered over according to abstract prescription nor simply avoided because we are afraid of the enormous work involved.

Contrasexuality emphasizes a paradox in gaining a secure sexual identity. In coming to terms with the unconscious archetypal contrasexual factor in ourselves—what Jung calls the anima in men and the animus in women—we become all the more a person of specific and workable sexual identity. We become more, not less, our own woman when we integrate the masculine components of our personality. The woman who comes to terms with her masculine side becomes fully and freely her own feminine being. She creatively improvises her identity from materials in her cultural conditioning and anatomy, but she is not herself solely determined by them. In integrating the animus archetype, a woman enlarges her sexual identity to include her own way of being and behaving in the "masculine" manner. Thus, she finds her own style of relating aggression, ambition, and determination to the so-called traditional feminine virtues of caring and concern.

The anima and animus are archetypes—that is, forms of readiness for response, without fixed contents. What they mediate to the ego as images of masculine and feminine is modified under the influence of culture. Jungians recognize that it is not only erroneous but clinically dangerous to assign fixed contents to the contrasexual factor, to equate anima with feeling or animus with thinking, for example. We need instead to observe closely what a particular woman's animus presents to her ego. Within the wide range of symbolism there exist distinct clusters of imagery associated with masculine and feminine, but we cannot assign set contents to the anima or animus of real persons. These must always be discovered in the concrete human situation.[2]

The result of integrating the contrasexual side of our natures is to heighten, deepen, and make more comfortably inhabitable our identities as women or men. A woman with her animus function integrated becomes more her own particular female self, radiating the life force which flows through her. Through the workings of this fuller sexuality and contrasexuality, she keeps in touch with the deep spiritual resources of her feminine being.

We especially need these resources in the church, particularly now with more women entering the ministry. Our faith has too long been parched, mechanical, prescriptive. We resort to ethical programs and political exhortation when we are estranged from the living center of religious experience. We need women who are connected to their feminine beings all the way deep down inside themselves, women who can communicate to the unconscious levels of being of their hearers rather than simply to a consciousness that is so often clouded with anger, arguments, fear, and resistance. Women can bring fresh insight to complex questions of the relation of sexuality to the symbolism of religious orders. We need not fall back into reactive positions that focus on male prejudice against the ordination of women. Instead, we can show forth feminine models and their relation to religious experience, already symbolically projected for Catholics, for example, in the dogma of the Assumption of Mary.

But to do this a woman needs to be securely and consciously anchored in her own feminine being. Paradoxically, this means consciously to receive her own masculine side. Without it, we lack the toughness to initiate new ways of being. On the other hand, if we allow the animus virtually to replace the ego's functions, we lose our own feminine identities.

WHAT IS THE ANIMUS?

The animus is a psychic complex that forms a bridge between a woman's conscious ego and the deeper layers of her unconsciousness. To function in a connected way is one of the chief hallmarks of the feminine. Heart and head cooperate so that at their best women have a capacity to generate a personal relatedness to their activities and spheres of work. The personal relatedness a woman feels to what she is doing or thinking brings into her activity what Heidegger calls the "caring mode." To the radical splits in our world between what we believe and how we act, this expression of care carries a healing effect. It is caring of a different quality from that seen in the efforts of modern bureaucracies that try to meet the needs of particular persons with an officious impersonality.

This connectedness operating in a woman helps her to harmonize disparate elements, such as the diverse personalities of her family, or the polarities of sexual and spiritual experience. The centrality of connectedness to the feminine is made poignantly clear in the pervasive distress we feel when disconnected. Then we feel eaten alive by the various needs and demands of our children, our husbands, our jobs, our friends. We know little success with schedules that compartmentalize our various tasks. When we do succeed in such compartmentalization—this hour for errands, that hour for lovemaking—our life's blood drains away. Resentment sets in. The atmosphere reeks with poisonous reproach or despair. We complain of feeling scattered, in pieces, confused—all symptoms that we have lost touch with a capacity for harmonious connectedness.

The animus functions to mediate contrasexual contents operating unconsciously in a woman's psyche to her ego, thus facilitating her capacity to focus upon them, to discriminate them from the men and the situations onto which she projects them. The animus performs this mediating function primarily by personifying the contents of the unconscious in images of manliness against which women measure actual men. One place we find these pictures is in our dreams. There, the animus personifies in male figures or masculine imagery images of impulses, needs, aspirations, or fantasies associated with the masculine that usually operate in us unconsciously.

Because the unconscious is comprised of personal, cultural, and archetypal layers, the animus brings up different types of pictures for conscious inspection.[3] Foremost are those of personal conditioning, derived from living experiences of the real men in a woman's life. Particularly influential are the actual men, a father, a brother, male figures of importance in earliest years, before a woman's ego is securely formed. The view her mother holds of men in the family and her mother's own animus are also very influential, for a little girl incorporates her mother's modes long before her own ego judgment takes shape.

In addition, the animus presents images to a woman of the male and masculine that are formed by cultural conditioning. These images operate just below the thresholds of our consciousness as anticipated patterns of behavior or emotional response that collective opinion ascribes to the male. Popular figures of sports, film, and the intellectual world are often held up as examples of what a "real" man is. Still deeper in the unconscious lie culturally influenced images of male authority associated with "truth and wisdom" in the symbol systems of science, art, and religion. Examples are great artists such as Rembrandt or Picasso, great national leaders such as Jefferson or Lincoln, great thinkers such as Plato or Augustine. All of them represent a kind of masculine authority.

More remote from consciousness are the impersonal, archaic,

and timeless images of the masculine such as penetrating light, overpowering force, form-creating energy. None is easily contained by verbal definition. Here the animus conveys an archetypal realm of the unconscious that transcends the specific conditioning of a given culture. It reaches back farther in time and more deeply into the unconscious to touch those images of elemental human experience that permeate all peoples' psyches everywhere. The following dreams of women illustrate the personal, cultural, and archetypal kinds of animus imagery. Often images from each level are mixed together, even within a single dream.

A woman dreams that an unknown man breaks into her apartment. Though she locks the door, the lock gives way as if this inanimate object were conspiring to admit the intruder. This typical dream at the very least conveys that some content outside the woman's consciousness wants to be made conscious. If she refuses it admittance, the chances are it will invade her in some violent way in the dream. The intruder, intent on robbing or raping her dream ego, may personify her own repressed sexual energy or unacknowledged aggression.

Dreams with blunt sexual content often mean that something in the dreamer's own unconscious is passionately seeking connection with the dreamer's ego. It might even force its way into her consciousness by trying to penetrate her defenses, trying to plant in her a seed of new life, a new way of looking at things. Jung described the animus as "a creative and procreative being, not in the sense of masculine creativity, but in the sense that he brings forth something we might call the *logos spermatikos*, the spermatic word."[4] Jung talks of the animus as "psychopomp"—a mediator that conducts unconscious contents to consciousness and thus helps the ego to discriminate regarding unconscious contents that are to be integrated. Thus the animus—always seen as male—is not a woman's soul or spirit. The animus is a psychic mechanism that facilitates connection to the contents of her unconscious, fishing up certain elements so that she can identify them and make use of them in her life instead of losing them in projections.

A second woman's dream illustrates how the animus may picture cultural bias against the female. Here something different happens. In graphic physical terms, the dream depicts a woman as completely acceptable. The dream corrects a cultural prejudice. "A group of Jews is to undergo a religious ceremony, some sort of rite of passage. I am allowed to join in, even though I am a Gentile and a woman. I know that in spite of these qualities I am entirely acceptable. . . . The ceremony is over. The rabbi comes and examines me to see if I am wearing a sanitary napkin. I am not, and do not have my period. 'Even if you had your period, it would have been all right,' he says. I know this is true in my heart. I feel that something very significant has taken place."

A third woman's dream illustrates the collective, archetypal imagery of the masculine. The dreamer discovers an ancient, numinous wise man. She dreams: "I am in a Victorian mansion. It has an infinite number of rooms, corridors, nooks, and crannies. Its complexity is beautiful and fascinating. At the very center, as in the center of a sphere, lives a sick, very old man. We [the dreamer and another woman] are going to see him. We unwrap him as from hundreds of layers of parchment, and he turns out to be quite robust, although he is very old. He is also infinitely wise, full of arcane information. He seems almost like God."

A fourth woman's dream presents an archaic image of the masculine, in the mythological form of a primitive reptile: "I stood next to my childhood summer home. Before me in the field opened a yawning hole in the ground. From it rose a gigantic serpent, primeval, awesome, like the ones you see swimming in the sea in illustrations for fairy tales." What stands out about this dream picture is the location of the serpent within the earth hole, suggesting a primordial form of masculine held in a feminine container; the two not yet differentiated.

THE SPLIT ANIMUS

It is no easy task to come to terms with all that an animus mediates to a woman's consciousness. Most of us find ourselves disconnected from the unconscious more often than connected. The notion of the split animus sums up the principal ways women get disconnected from their own unconscious contrasexual resources and do not receive the masculine elements of their personalities.[5] Instead of mediating unconscious contents to consciousness, the animus seems to be falling away from consciousness and the ego pulling away from the animus. The bridge seems to be collapsing from both sides.

Like any other archetype, the animus is collective in nature and impelled by impersonal unconscious energies that stir up attendant emotional and behavioral reaction patterns. The animus is not part of a woman's subjective ego territory. It is a bridge to the collective world of the unconscious. When it is *not* functioning adequately, it is personified as if the unconscious were trying to show what attitude needs to be integrated in order to establish connection between the conscious and unconscious.

A frequent misunderstanding of the animus ascribes to it a set stereotyped content, unchanging in all women and in all cultures, as if Jung meant to say that the animus consisted of immutable masculine characteristics. It is not so. The *function* of connecting ego and unconscious images associated with the masculine is similar in different women; the *content* varies according to personal experience, cultural conditioning, and the archetypes of the masculine concretized in a given woman's psychology. There are, however, certain dysfunctions of the animus that set off serious problems for most women. These typical disturbances gather around emotional possession, intellectual identification, split authority, and a kind of sexual problem that is best called that of the "girl-matron."

EMOTIONAL POSSESSION

Emotional possession takes familiar forms to most of us. We feel invaded by an emotion-laden energy that dominates our behavior. We run roughshod over other persons' conversations. We must drive our point home, even if we have to harangue our listener to do so. Or, full of outrage at our husband's criticism, we leap into argument, prosecuting his past failures and his general unfairness. Or, flooded by waves of hurt and disbelief at the obtuseness of our lover's questions about our past, we sink into a stunned silence that covers our steely refusal to answer. Or, tensely alert to defend our dearly held position, we scan our teacher with sullen eye, waiting to pounce at any sign of a view we may find disagreeable or at variance with ours in any way. When the argument is joined, we know no bounds. We run wildly ahead, reckless of the welfare of others. Unable to restrain ourselves, we drop our bombs. We goad others with shrill tones. We enrage them with a passive resistance seething with unvoiced reproach. We exhaust their patience, so that finally they must throw up their hands in disgust. We are completely out of reach. Their resultant dismissal of us only confirms us in our frenzied isolation. We feel misunderstood. We are misunderstood. We misunderstand. We are hurt. Above all, we are spent, as if tossed by a great windstorm that has rushed through us, and between us and the others. We feel thrown down, uprooted, bruised.

This is how it feels to be invaded by an animus force rather than connected to it. Instead of channeling the unconscious energy the animus brings, we go under before its onslaught. Our egos are overtaken. They abandon the scene. Impersonal unconscious en-

ergy swamps our ego concerns. This can be dangerous. We feel
possessed, compelled to activities that we know will thwart what
we hold most dear, but we plunge on, carried by a current stronger
than our own will. We can even act violently, against ourselves or
others. The unconscious breaks in and dominates the ego. The
splitting of ego and animus leaves our unconscious energies with
no conscious use in everyday life, and leaves the ego without
energy to pursue its own goals and values.

Falling into a secondary position, the passive ego comprises the
key to all kinds of animus possession. Where the ego should be,
a vacuum exists. The animus rushes in, uncontained, unchanneled, impersonal. The ego feels victimized and tends to project
the danger outward, endowing others with victimizing intent.
This projection is aided by present-day ferment about the liberation of women from second-class status. These real injustices act
as perfect hooks for the projection of inward feelings of persecution. Then we feel besieged from both sides. Externally, we are the
victims of sexist prejudice; internally, the victims of animus domination. Further pressure is caused by men who project their own
feminine sides outward onto women, whom they then invariably
identify with those projections.[6] In all these cases, women do not
receive themselves and are not received as they actually are, but
are always viewed instead through a screen of unconscious projections from others and from within themselves, through the animus.

THE ANIMA AND WOMEN

Projection onto women by men happens most frequently in
professions where women are excluded from equal footing with
men. When no woman's presence is really felt, the contrasexual
anima factor in men tends to build up as if to compensate for the
outward lack. However, the contrasexual element always differs

significantly from conscious sexual identity in the opposite sex. The femininity of the anima, for example, is not the same as the femininity displayed in the personalities of actual women.

Problems arise when men think women duplicate the characteristics of their own anima and therefore deserve the same treatment or mistreatment given to their anima. The anima lacks the vital force of the female; it is, after all, only a component part of the male personality and hence more passive and properly secondary to male ego functioning. If men project their animas onto women they unconsciously assume that women's place in the world is also secondary. Lacking the ruthless potential of a real woman, the man's anima tends to be more sentimental than women are, more given to vanity and softheadedness. Thus men say one thing and do another. They vote "yes" when in fact they believe "no," because they fear others' dislike or that they may hurt someone or get hurt if they follow their conscience. They may do more harm to others as well as themselves by betraying their conscience, but the blame is spread around and not clearly located at their door. Whereas if they were to stand up and say "no" outright, they could be criticized.

A particularly good example of lack of anima toughness turns up in some men's responses to the women's movement. These men enthusiastically agree with feminist claims, consciously accept their own guilt en masse, as a sex, for the mistreatment of women. But what they give with one hand, they withhold with the other. The man who indulges in abstractions of guilt fails to pay his cleaning lady a decent wage, or to share in the housework with his wife. Unconsciously he remains untouched in his basic attitudes. He plugs publicly for rights of women, but do not expect him to clear the table. When he gets a job offer, the family must move, despite the uprooting of his wife's career.

Another example of a man under the sway of the anima is seeing a woman as a mere sex object. Breasts, bottoms, and genital parts as well, stare at the viewer from the glossy girlie magazines, but the male reader rarely treats an actual woman's sexual parts with such intense scrutiny or loving inspection. Women in the abstract, yes; woman in the concrete, no. Without real women, this tendency to sentimentalize may go unchecked, a problem often seen in the church.

The rise of anima femininity may also account in some circumstances for the appearance of homosexuality. Men begin to live out of their contrasexual side at the expense of their conscious masculine adaptation. This occurs in part to supply the feminine presence missing from the scene, and in part because the anima does not receive adequate attention from the ego and swamps it. The women's movement shows a corresponding rise of attraction to lesbianism. The contrasexual side of women's personalities accumulates in an all-female atmosphere and some women come to live out of it more than from their conscious female identities, especially if they cannot easily receive their reality as females.

INTELLECTUAL IDENTIFICATION

A woman's split animus condition frequently appears in intellectual terms. Her ego once again gets invaded by the unconscious contents the animus would mediate to consciousness. Instead of receiving these, sorting them out, and using them, the ego identifies with ready-made, unexamined, taken-for-granted opinions that a woman utters as if they were indisputable facts that everyone knows.

The personal root of the contrasexual animus in a woman's psyche reaches to her introjected images of her father or of significant men in her life, and often, also, the very men who have shaped her mother's animus. For example, a mother with her own father complex hands down to her daughter accounts of the superior exploits and sterling qualities of the child's grandfather. There is more—the dominant cultural images of masculine authority contribute a great deal to the formation of her animus. A woman easily identifies with the accumulated collections of conventional masculine opinions, from father on down, and just as easily projects her identifications onto the world around her.[7]

Masculine opinions operate in a woman's psyche as a layer of *assumed* truths, though she may be barely conscious of them as such. On the basis of these assumptions, she pronounces her views on any question at hand. She treats her assumptions as facts, in the sense that they describe the fixed dimensions of her world view. Unconsciously, she experiences them as intrinsically connected to the person she is in her most essential self. Thus if others challenge these opinions or simply refer to them as "mere assumptions," she feels deeply upset, even violated. This explains her vitriolic arguments against those who do not identify with her views. She feels they are attacking her at the core of her being, and so she defends herself like a cornered animal. In the resultant confusion, the priceless insight that is there to be uncovered will almost certainly be lost. These opinions, instead of being swallowed whole and mouthed again as dicta—which happens when we identify with them—should be received as inherited information, as shaping guidelines, as added knowledge for use in forming our own viewpoint for ourself. In no way should they structure the center of our being.

In religious circles, to take a strong example, a woman may feel dominated by patriarchal views of the feminine, which she assumes everyone around her holds. She then reacts to religious tradition as if it could be defined as nothing but patriarchal sexism. This assumption demoralizes her, saps the strength she needs to fight discrimination where it really does exist. She fails to gather support from those elements that really exist in her religion. Moreover, she is extremely vulnerable to new opinions she agrees with, which she will quickly accept as true. Some members of the women's movement give the impression that they alone know the truth. But the truth of sisterhood does not hold up under the onslaught of animus domination. Animus-driven sisters treat those women who do not identify absolutely and totally with the cause as they define it as the enemy, to be ostracized, to be persecuted. The woman dominated by ready-made truths reduces herself to a machine. No matter what question is put to her, what issue raised, she inevitably pins a "sexist" label on it. Put a nickel in, get a sexist prescription out. The woman becomes a mere ideologue. Ironically, when a woman fights this way against the external prejudice that would make women inferior to men, she falls victim internally to another version of this same prejudice. As a result she fails ever to discover her own ideas, distinct from the collective weight of either old or new authority.

THE ANIMUS AND MEN

Just as the anima's femininity differs from that of actual women, so the masculine qualities of the animus differ from those of actual men. Like the anima, the unconnected animus partakes of a fuzzy abstractionism. Women dominated by unconscious animus assumptions sound platitudes that presumably convince by force rather than by accuracy or relevance to the issue at hand. They speak for "truth," for "the right thing," and "what people think." Genuine objectivity does not characterize animus opinions. The ability to speculate about facts, to see them in this arrangement or that, in order to stimulate new ideas, disappears. A great stake attaches to the outcome of the argument, because unconsciously a woman identifies with her assumptions, even though she may be unclear about what they are. If one disagrees with her conclusions, the very foundations of her being are shaken. Therefore, she must steer the argument along predefined lines. The argument cannot develop freely; the woman must control it.

Something is always being proved. Nothing different can be discovered. We must arrive at clear validation of the point as defined by the animus-dominated woman. The result is that she loses touch with the real issues she wanted to explore and fails to bring forward her own insight or make her own feminine viewpoint really present.

In its intellectual form, this unconscious identification with the animus produces painful situations for a woman. We frequently hear women's thinking characterized as second-rate, full of clichés or lacking originality. When these criticisms prove true—and sometimes they do—it is usually because all the pieces of our reactions have not been connected. We have not structured our own viewpoint.

Take the experience of reading a theorist we particularly like because the author verbalizes perceptions we dimly discern to be true. The author's ideas connect with our own, reaching us where we live in our feelings as well as where we do our thinking. We may learn with dismay, however, that when we discuss this author's theory we exude fogginess, and a mumbo-jumbo sort of emotion, full of enthusiasm but totally without critical judgment. Instead of honoring the author we admire with our own understanding, we copy the author slavishly.[8] When someone points this out to us, we feel hurt, stunned, as if something in us had been struck down.

What happens is that our egos unconsciously identify with the ideas we admire. Swallowing those ideas *en bloc*, without sorting through them and above all trying to discover what we really think about them, we begin to talk at a secondary level. We have been living off someone else's intellectual land, instead of finding our own ground of thought. Clearly, we owe debts to our teachers and to other authorities for what they teach us, but we need not become their parrots. Jung does not see the unconscious "as one big bag, or a black hole full of water"[9] but rather as possessed of "stories or layers"; hence his famous use of the house of many levels as a metaphor for the psyche. The animus has its own layers.

Beneath the tiers of influence of our parents and the culture around us, there lies, according to Jung, an autonomous *a priori* existence of the unconscious out of which ego functioning emerges. Beneath the animus of a woman's personality there lies a primordial spiritual force that drives us toward articulation of meanings. This considerable force arises from the deep collective layers of a woman's unconscious and can lead her to receive her own Self (for Jung the center of the psyche), which for women often manifests itself in unmistakably female form.[10] We must receive into consciousness this deep impulse toward meaning as the basis for constructing a sense of values in relationships with others.

Any woman whose thought matures will develop a capacity to think for herself—to put together bits and pieces of insight in a disciplined way. This frees her to receive spontaneous intuitions of her point of view from beneath the surface of her life. She comes to connect her lived experience with some conception of its meaning and the spirit that informs it. She thinks with her own authority, rather than as an intellectual groupie who merely copies whatever outside authority declares to be true.

SPLIT AUTHORITY

When we are animus possessed, our sense of authority is as split as our inmost being. Unconnected emotions rush through our egos instead of becoming humanized and put at our disposal as feelings. We unconsciously fall into identifications with others' ideas, parroting them as our own. Our authority does not take its roots in the depths of our own being, connecting consciousness and the unconscious. Instead we paste on authoritative words, slogans from the outside. We protest that we want our own authority, but we draw a blank on what it actually is. We do not know exactly where we stand, what we think, how we actually feel. Essentially we remain in a passive, secondary position, awaiting a stimulus outside our consciousness to act as a prime mover.

A split in authority produces two equally unattractive opposite extremes. In each the ego remains in a secondary position, with the projected animus standing in front of it in first place. Either we simply go on in our unconscious identification with inherited authority, or in defiance we seize control and will brook no interference with our own posture. In the first state, we let someone else—father, mother, husband, church, or movement—carry the authority for us. We do as they say or we may rebel against and subvert what they prescribe. In either case the authority remains out there, not drawn from our own experience. We persist in reacting only, never initiating. Usually our behavior sets up a love-hate relationship to this authority. We refer to it, we seek it out for advice, like a father figure always in the background. But if the advice displeases us, we complain of being hectored and bewail an insensitive meddling, a manipulative intrusion.

In the second alternative we cast off all outside authorities, as if unconscious identification could simply be repudiated instead of understood and worked through. In fact, we exchange a former authority figure for our own image of authority. We find ourselves possessed by this image, inflated by its unconscious energy, exchanging a previous formlessness for an equally empty rigidity of position.

We need to receive into awareness a firmness of personal conviction where we know what we know and stand on it for definite reasons, knowing too that we can change if our perceptions or thoughts change. This sort of authority organizes and connects our experience and thought, joins listening to others with arriving at our own conclusions. Such authority can grow strong without being defensive and can take on personal definition.

We achieve our authority on the basis of actual experience. Through reflection we connect to our sense of who we are, where we have been, and where we are going. Thus we are neither amorphous nor rigid, but anchored in what we have lived through and thought about. Behind that rests our reception of the tradition, what others have said in the accumulated knowledge of culture. There is no substitute for this sort of personal experience which gives us a secure and fertile place to root a new cultural tradition. We join up with aspects of collective experience to which we have access through the particular details of our own personal experience. As we do, we discover that we only have significant access to our experience through the tutoring of a cultural tradition to which we have a strong connection. Thus our authority is a capacity to stand firmly *behind* what we say and to say what we believe. Intimate connection to our own personal experience *and* to collective human experience gives us that capacity to beget connections with and for others. Such authority engenders respect for other's experience and allows us to be open and at the same time clearly defined. Our openness becomes a personal openness as contrasted with an undefined open-endedness where one simply has not achieved any real point of view.

Two different examples may serve as illustrations. The first example was given to me by a middle-aged woman, who told about her first experience in childbirth over twenty years ago. She put herself in the doctor's hands, relying on his wisdom to bring her and her expected child through. She also sought classes in natural childbirth, an unorthodox thing to do in those days. The teacher urged upon her this "better" way as more in keeping with her female instincts in contrast to her male doctor's and modern medicine's man-made procedures for bringing a child into the world. When the time came for her to give birth, the doctor predicted a long labor and left her in the labor room to go about other business. She felt in her body that he was wrong. Her teacher had warned her of such possibility and instructed her in detail how to give birth on her own. The woman, however, felt cowed by neither authority. Her body's contractions told her the doctor might be wrong. Her knowledge of her own personality told her she did not want to "show" him by going on alone without benefit of medical support if needed. So she spoke up loudly for what she thought was right. She insisted the baby was coming soon. While she used her teacher's helpful instructions to aid the process, she insisted on a medical backup team to help her if needed. She followed her own authority and brought a healthy baby into the world.

The second example is taken from theology. Valerie Goldstein published a short essay on sin from a woman's point of view that stood traditional interpretations on their heads. For a woman sin is not pride, an exaltation of self, but a refusal to claim the self God has given. Women refuse this self by hiding behind self-doubt and feelings of inadequacy.[11] The force of her argument arises from countless women's experience of avoiding the self that they are, by always assuming that some greater authority knows better, be that father, mother, husband, even, in this case, theologians' interpretation of sin.

In both examples, something authentic is expressed that does not shout down other's views, but takes what is useful from them to form an original view helpful to all of us.

THE GIRL-MATRON

The split animus condition affects a woman's sexual identity, her sense of being a woman. It creates what I have called a "girl-matron." We have seen that the animus is many-layered. It conveys to a woman's ego personal unconscious material such as the influences of others and experiences of early childhood. It also brings alive nonpersonal archetypal images of the masculine. This nonpersonal aspect of the animus mediates a primordial sense of the spirit residing in her unconscious beneath the influence of personal father figures and cultural authorities. This sense of spirit is part of her feminine self and is felt by her as the intimation of value for the sake of which she risks becoming conscious. She leaves behind her the comfortable recurrent cycles of simple physical existence, taking experience as it comes, never linking it up to consciousness, falling into endless rounds of hunger and satiation, sleep and activity, and desire and gratification.[12] The animus mediates spiritual aspiration in the form of images that inspire her somehow, consciously, to construct a system of values, reaching for purpose and meaning in life. One woman felt she had glimpsed a truth that she never knew existed until she heard a particular lecturer. She felt a sense of "being called," of "touching another dimension," something "terribly important" that she must "digest" and make her own. She projected her animus upon the lecturer.

Some of us struggle to avoid this task. We stay in a pre-animus phase where we do not receive the spiritual function into consciousness, but continue to project it onto others. Let them carry it, we say. We prefer to remain girls, dependent on wiser ones to point the way. Avoiding the turmoil and drudgery involved in trying to establish our own connection to the spiritual dimension strongly affects our sexual life. We become the "girl-matron" that Americans know so well. We pass from being a child-to-a-parent to becoming a parent-to-a-child either literally or figuratively, without fully receiving our adult womanhood. Though we may have given birth to several children, may have known many lovers, it is as if we have never been penetrated spiritually with the seeds of living connection to metaphysical being. We lack adult sexuality. We lack a center. Regardless of physical attractiveness, a central vitality is missing. The power of our physical sexual presence is diluted. That part of our sexuality which connects with the spirit remains unlived. We seem still to be one of the girls. We avoid differentiating the masculine and feminine aspects of our own personality, leaving them instead a pleasant blur or an unpleasant confusion. We have not become our own kind of women, secure in what it means to be female with developed and usable "masculine" capacities as well. By avoiding any significant differentiation of male and female, we either force ourselves into exclusively female roles where we compulsively unite with members of the other sex to make up a heterosexual unit, or into antimale roles such as a militant lesbianism.

Other forms of avoidance of the spiritual come from opposite directions. Instead of grown-up girls now turned matrons, we may become aging tomboys. We may avoid sexual relations altogether, extending forever the buddy ideal or brother-sister model of relations. Or we may play at sex without letting it evoke our own inward responses. We may imitate a pseudo-masculine sexuality— a spasmodic sex with changing partners that, whatever its physical expression, remains confined within an autoerotic circle. We eliminate our desire in sexual encounters as if it were only just so much accumulated tension, an internal riddance mirrored in the external rapid discarding of sexual partners. Even with a steady partner, the stimulating source of our arousal may stay lodged in our own fantasy rather than in response to the actual person. Consciously or unconsciously we do not enjoy our own feminine mode of being a sexual person. The animus does not operate within us to connect us to our feminine reality, but is lived instead on the outside as a pseudo-masculine adaptation. The feminine ego takes a back seat.[13]

RECEIVING THE ANIMUS: HUMANIZING UNCONSCIOUS ENERGY

The animus complex connects a woman's ego to the unconscious contents of her contrasexual nature. The animus stands with one foot in the personal unconscious—introjected images of actual males in a woman's life, other dominant images of the masculine in her particular culture, and all those drives and impulses that a particular woman herself associates with the masculine aspects of her personality. The other foot of the animus stands in the collective unconscious, that *a priori* dimension of psychic process that precedes and gives rise to the conscious ego. What is found here does not originate in introjected objects from the outside world, but arises as images, fantasies, and undifferentiated ideas of the elemental human experience of the masculine. The unconscious presents itself as impersonal and nonhuman in contrast to the memories, fears, and desires of the first type of unconscious material. Here, animus images are usually archaic rather than reflective of civilized experience. A woman may be confronted in a dream by a primordial phallus, for example, or an ancient warrior lusting for battle. The animus may mediate to a woman's ego awareness in great gusts of emotion, or in compelling drives that she does not feel as properly her own, but rather as energy rushing through her. This may happen when she meets a new man who attracts her. Just as easily it may occur when she hits on a creative idea, a new plan of action, or a spiritual insight. Our task is to personalize this energy by building a conscious relation to it. This is the hard work involved in transforming unconscious energy into usable human forms.

Humanizing unconscious energy means bringing it into ego-consciousness, with its warmth of feeling and its pervading human values. To do this demands imagination. We must devise some special kinds of conversation, give-and-take interchanges between what we consciously value and what this rush of unconscious energy would impel us to do. For a woman it means learning to hold her ground inside herself against the force of collective nonpersonal unconscious drives. She must gradually mix with them, modifying and taming them for clearly channeled uses. In our time this task of transformation has become crucial. For our accepted channels of spiritual guidance and of cultural forms for men and women *as* men and women are all being challenged. As a result, women feel both hopelessly confused and pressed to find new ground on which to stand.[14] To find their own feminine authority women discover that they must connect to the elemental apprehension of spirit deep within their feminine being.

Connection is needed, both to the upswelling of unconscious, unformed spiritual energy, on the one hand, and to the world of shared existence among people on the other. The point of connection in the woman between these two worlds of inner unconscious life and outer society is her own small human ego.

There is no better preparation for facing collective forces in the outside world than this exercise of ego-clarification used to confront collective unconscious forces within the psyche. This kind of work equips us to hear both the voiced and unvoiced oppositions of other people to our goals—without our automatically reacting with hurt, anger, and impatience. In learning to build a bridge to the unconscious in ourselves, we learn to connect with the unconscious of others. In learning to receive what unconscious contents the animus conveys, we learn to receive unvoiced messages from the unconscious of others. We are less apt to project our inner critic onto our outer one, thus doubling his critical strength, for example, and more apt to perceive that he projects part of himself onto us, without falling into identification with that projection. Our strength then comes from within ourselves and gives us real security. We stand on what we value and develop a capacity to relate value to ever new unconscious material that crosses into consciousness. From a human point of view, our greater receptiveness promotes what might be seen as an incarnating process that must continue in us, gradually transforming the stuff of the psyche into human consciousness, caring the world into being.

The church, also, stands on a frontier between undifferentiated and hence unchanneled psychic energy and the needs of the world. The number of commercially successful films about natural disasters makes one wonder what unconscious message they are unwittingly portraying. Earthquakes, tidal waves, outbreaks of raging fire, atomic disasters, swarming insects, man-eating sharks all describe the rising up of powerful forces of nature that must break in and overcome our human communities. We may speculate that such natural forces portray the onslaught of unconscious psychic energy that threatens our collective and individual ego world. Without sufficient numbers of persons who can consciously relate on their own to the great forces amassing in the collective unconscious, these films may presage a real disaster that will in fact overtake us.[15] Our century has known many such outbreaks of collective frenzy that smash not only the values of being human, but all capacity even to see the human person, much less understand it.

The church plays a preventive and transformative role with respect to the collective unconscious. It acts as a kind of demilitarized zone between the unformed forces of spiritual aspiration and the life of civilized values. In prayers, in ritual, in liturgy, communities of people partake of mixtures of conscious and unconscious processes in contained forms that are sometimes magnificent. At the heart of the Eucharist is the instinct of cannibalism. Mixed with prayer is childish wish fulfillment. Mixed with celebrations of joyous triumph is the stark reality of suffering. Permeating a worship service on a Sunday morning is the aura of timelessness, stretching back beyond human history and forward to include death, with all the terrors of each boundaryless epoch. Instinct in religious life is an openness to the unbound, uncontained, nonrational, and nonlogical apprehension of being.

The church makes room for unconscious life when it allows unconscious reception and inflow, not in chaotic ways, but in roomy systems of thought and practice that permit us to live in close proximity to unconscious forces without being destroyed by them. This permission, this space-making, relieves some of the collective unconscious pressure in our shared atmosphere, and thus the church intercedes on behalf of the values of humanity with the archaic forces of life and death. But the church goes further and may act as a place of transformation where this unconscious energy finds channels to bring it into life, so that it can support life instead of threatening it.

From the church we learn that all of our humanity is acceptable, even that which is not yet humanized. We learn of the grace of God's presence to us and within us, acting as a center which can summon us inside ourselves toward the integration of the different split parts of our personalities into an indivisible whole. It can summon us in outer ceremonies to unite our fractured world into a network of justice-serving societies. The church stands witness to the Word of God in human form in the figure of Jesus Christ. Thus it brings the collective currents of psychic energy into relation with the central Word. It relativizes this energy as just another medium of the central truth about existence, however powerful. It proclaims the fact that such energies are created and finds their center only in relation to their Creator. The unconscious energies then can find a connecting point with personal, human life-forms, to flow into human existence through the agency of the person and figure of Jesus Christ. The church makes God's presence known in this way, using its human agents to do so. Women who would speak as priests commissioned with the authority of the church must also be anchored in their own female human authority, and not be swept away by every gust of unconscious reaction from within or every new social pressure from without.

FROM DISCONNECTION TO CONNECTION: WOMAN'S PRESENCE

Given the history of bias against women and the current over-turning of laws and attitudes that confine women to second-class status, most women today know the convulsive effects of a dysfunctional animus, whether or not they know this psychological terminology. One way we experience this rupture is in the push and pull between the feminine and masculine sides of ourselves. The quite simply defined struggles of our grandmothers and great-grandmothers between work and home have yielded now to many more possibilities of the joining of career and family—and of disjunction. Our struggle, even if more internalized, is no less severe because we are trying to bring together into some sort of pattern all of our capacities to be and to do in our world. We must move, however convulsively, from a state of disconnection toward connection. We cannot simply start out at the end point. What I say here bears a rough correlation to the split animus disconnections mentioned above and should be thought of in association with them.

The sexual issue in particular is addressed when we move to mend the different kinds of splits that separate emotion and mind. In each linking up of the elements that were disconnected a woman will pour into her center of being more and more psychic and physical energy, and that will in turn establish new channels for instinctive response. She can now yield her body calmly to her own desire and put it comfortably into the hands of her sexual partner, for now she has a sense of self out of which she can give and receive. She can really feel a man to be an agent of love when she gives up her negative projections onto him such as robber, rapist, or weakling.

When we are possessed by the inrush of unconscious instinct, emotion, or ideas, our egos fall captive to animus domination. We open our mouths and "it" speaks, mouthing words and emotions that are generally valid but which do not specifically relate to the immediate issue or person at hand. We are often vulnerable to this sort of possession because of a vacuum in our conscious standpoint. Where there should be a conscious feeling or attitude, a blank exists instead. The unconscious rushes in. The animus wants —so to speak—to bring to our conscious attention the unconscious material out of which we can formulate our own attitude, but the animus cannot do that work for us. Hence when a vacuum exists instead of our ego receiving this unconscious material, all the unconscious energy simply rushes in. Our own particular animus complex persists in enunciating a stubborn bias that is impervious to any influence of fact, person, or logic. Our ego no longer centers our consciousness. It has fallen into the unconscious. Instead, the animus plays the ego part, for which it is not adapted. And thus we strike others as opinionated, frenzied, or insistent.

We need to learn to focus on and receive into consciousness all these materials the animus wants to hand us—opinions, advice, reactions, memories. We need to know that all this unconscious stuff is operating within us, and that it will only too easily spout out of us, spinning its webs of illusion around us, so that we do not see the other person or the other issue or even our own personal reactions. We form no genuine point of view this way; we come up only with borrowed ones. Now we must somehow tell the animus messenger of the unconscious what our personal ego-bound feelings, hopes, and values are. We must inform our unconscious of our conscious point of view.

This double focusing on what the animus brings and what the ego brings takes us into ourselves, initiating a journey down into our unconscious roots. It makes an outward effect a real presence. We may discover, for example, that these borrowed opinions stem from the influence of various men in our lives, from father to our most recent male connection. Or they may come from the undigested opinions of significant women in our lives. Some have assaulted us so strongly that they shout forth in us and from us, not imbued with a particular female's quality of thought, but simply proclaiming the "truth," all the more insistently roared at the world as they remain unassimilated.

We may discover that instead of asserting our own female point of view, we have been replicating the masculine by speaking so harshly through the animus. We see this in the women who fight against male domination while unwittingly adopting the style of that domination. To win on the outside and be defeated on the inside is worth nothing. To be obsessed with power and superiority and scheming strategies is merely to replay the worst of what has been attacked as patriarchal sin. We rely too much on words and verbal battle, when only touching our opponents' *unconscious* fear of the female could help. If we are out of touch with our own unconscious, there is no way we can get in touch with another's except destructively.

In looking at what the animus mediates to our egos we may begin to see what lies behind this assemblage of fathers operating within us.[16] Those unconscious assumptions with which we have identified intellectually mask a blank space within us. Precisely there we need to formulate a point of view and exercise ego value judgment. We need to receive into consciousness bits and pieces of our own reactions, responses, intuitions, and thoughts and gradually to construct our individual point of view. In this carefully crafted viewpoint we remain open to reality factors. We no longer need unconsciously to defend assumptions that must be right because a parental figure said they were, or, conversely, because we must defy parental authority.

Through hints, images, readings, cultural currents, our own experience, and efforts to think out a position, we begin to experience the real fathering spirit of the unconscious.[17] We know that pivotal impulse toward living with meaning and direction in which all of our personality flourishes. Jung writes: "These are the truths that speak to the soul which are not too loud and do not insist too much, but reach the individual in stillness."[18] These truths fertilize new life in a woman, bringing her to the point where she is capable of some strong manifestation of spirit. In touch with other persons, we may act as agents of regeneration in our own world. This proper functioning of the animus helps us to live open lives, and through ourselves to extend to other people around us a deeper source of authority. This is what is described in archetypal images as the mana of the feminine, a source that engenders new mixtures of flesh and spirit, of the human and the divine.[19]

Women priests or ministers must first be open to the touch of the spirit if they are to bring into religion the spirit as it touches them. Even in the crucial issue of the ordination of women, we must not get caught in prejudiced conclusions about how issues should turn out. We must allow for the workings of the spirit. This does not mean following that "meek and mild" image so often pinned onto the figure of Mary, portraying her as a woman without any passion or anger. It means conceiving the issues surrounding the ordination of women and the styles of their ministry, whether lay or ordained, as a deep risk-taking, fully open to God's way. This may lead to styles of ministry we have never dreamed of—or perhaps have only glimpsed in dreams, seeing behind text and doctrine the workings of the spirit.

ATTENDING TO EGO WOUNDS

To restore the animus function as a bridge between contrasexual unconscious material and the feminine ego-identity requires a double focus. We must look at both the ego's world of personal feelings and values and at the archaic images, introjected opinions, and authority figures that the animus personifies. Impersonal unconscious energies need to be connected to personal concerns, and ready-made animus opinions need to be examined and either as-similated or discarded by the ego as it constructs its own views. In each instance the ego must gradually fill a vacuum, thus depriving the animus energies of an unconscious outlet.

Another broken connection between ego and animus occurs when the ego suffers a wound that has been repressed. The unrecognized hurt creates a blank space of nonreaction in the functioning of the ego. Where there should be conscious response, a hiatus exists. This deep wound is the result of direct and indirect attacks on a woman's sexual identity and self-esteem as a female. The wound is kept festering by general prejudice against the female sex. She never can be sure when she might be excluded from a job, from full participation in community life, or from another person's mind or feelings simply because she is a woman.

The uprush of feeling from the unconscious takes all the forms of emotional possession discussed earlier. We heap accusations and gnash our teeth in fury over our own scorned sex. The girl-matron phenomenon is due in part to this prejudice against the female. For to be a girl or a matron is a way to stay on the safe outer sides of the chasm between girlhood and maturity. The vibrantly alive and sexually functioning adult female holds nothing back, neither the faults nor the virtues, but wants to give and receive all.

To be able to receive another this way, we must fully receive ourselves. That means no longer ignoring our wounds but being willing to look right at them and to feel their pain and acknowledge it. When our feelings are hurt in this most personal area of our self-esteem, most of us do not register the extent of the hurt we suffered, but rather let it fall into the unconscious. We fail then to assert a personal reaction. The animus takes over in place of the ego with attacks of vengeful affect toward others and reproaches against ourselves as well. Bitterness, resentment, and stubbornness capture us.

The accumulation of hurt feeling is important to receive into awareness. We need constantly to feel it, register it, suffer it, so that our system can be cleansed. Otherwise we simply pile hurt upon hurt until we develop that hardness of heart which leaves us incapable of feeling anything. We must feel the pain and weep so that the pain does not conquer us.

This is once again a matter of focusing. We turn from the stiff shield that has blocked off accumulated pain and look at it directly, inside ourselves and outside. This strong look at our hurt can produce a softening reconciliation within ourselves that may protect us from stiffening our defensive postures. More than anything else, this sort of softening is needed to make us more strongly felt in our world. It comes from motions of inward love toward our own unconscious hurts and damaged self-esteem that will allow us as women to connect our work with our love, so that the work we do is inspired work because it is undertaken for love.

This sort of grounding of feeling in our deepest unconscious roots allows us to direct our rage against life-destroying bureaucracies and institutionalized attitudes in a way that serves life and abets positive change. Accepting our own pain permits us to be clear and unsentimental but not unfeeling about the real hardships of life. We thus acquire more of the compassion that resists rushing in with political slogans and illegitimate power grabs. We can stand with those who suffer and do something to ease their misery because we have stood with our own suffering.

THE FEMININE PRESENCE

Combinations of these ways of restoring the animus function will connect our womanly egos to the contrasexual roots in the unconscious. Thus we put together the masculine and feminine parts of ourselves. By keeping the animus informed of our personal feelings and values, and by paying attention to the unconscious assumptions, attitudes, and convictions that the animus portrays to us, we connect our unconscious energies to our conscious values and feelings with a strong life-giving warmth. Thus, bit by bit, we personalize some of the impersonal energies residing unconsciously around us. These unconscious energies can find new outlets, like water seeping into the ground, facilitating the growth of new thoughts, establishing a fertile spiritual atmosphere that will allow new perceptions to grow and take shape all around us.

By focusing on what we know, and knowing that we know it, by asserting the authority of our own experience instead of parroting others, we bring what we know into articulate expression. We can put what we know now at the disposal of consciousness, our own and others'.

We make available views of life from a feminine perspective, a perspective the world needs very much. We express this perspective clearly and responsibly, no longer content to hope—or fear—that others will somehow intuit what we mean.

By turning to our own pain, and fully receiving it, we do not stuff it away to burst forth sometime, uncontrollably. Getting over our pain, we resist the temptation to despair over the cruelty we all do to each other. We create an enabling space where others may allow their feelings to reach consciousness too.[20]

This clear receiving of our own responses affects our sexuality directly and positively. At less than conscious levels women fear being hurt if they permit themselves to open totally to their own desires and to their love for another. So their sexuality has a fearful and negative edge to it. Receiving themselves brings security. Security modifies fear and helps transmute it into a receptive yielding to another, enhanced by a quivering excitement that is like the tremblings of fear, though it is in fact just the opposite. Good sexual experience acquaints a woman directly with the satisfaction and self-esteem her adult sexuality deserves. In this sexual vibrancy she is rescued from the defenses of girl-matronhood and becomes through all her new softening connections a tough-spirited woman.

This toughness creates a receptiveness of atmosphere where things can happen around a woman. Ideas take root. People feel more possible. Imagination discovers new images. The church needs from its women a fertilizing of the ground, a mixing of its traditions with new insights.

Some may complain that such an approach must take too long. The argument does not hold up. For when something grows this way, with its own tough, tangible presence, it has staying power. It does not fall exhausted from the battle, conquered from within by what it has fought without.

7

Woman Receiving

All women have a special ministry, not only those who become priests and ministers of the church. Women must throw off the roles so long projected upon them and carry on their historic struggle to receive and to be received as persons, to *be* at the core, concretely, as persons. They must refuse to be seen as an abstraction or a type, to be drawn from the tight compartments of sociological classification.

This insistence on receiving herself can take many forms for a woman. One woman in analysis who worked through unconscious ties to her childhood dreamed that "it was necessary to kill my mother and then chop her up into little pieces. It was simply something that had to be done, a necessary task, rather than a terrible sadness or an act of violence." Another woman found her professional career blocked by the highly charged, ambivalent emotions that she directed toward her former supervisor. One day, standing before his desk and feeling emotional turmoil creep over her once again, she suddenly took a conscious stand against always giving her authority over to this supervisor. Talking to herself, she said: "I can't give my life's blood to feed him anymore. I must feed myself with my own work." The image of blood touches the archetypal theme where a woman's life energy is sacrificed to feed a demon lover. Here, happily, a reversal occurred and the woman recovered her own center of authority.

Where our Judeo-Christian tradition has grown pallid, our faith dry and lacking in self-renewal, it is because we have lost the sense of human presence, and with the human presence, the divine as well. The personal, concrete God promised to be with us wherever two or three are gathered in Christ's name. Having lost our centering points, we flounder hopelessly. Some of us return to the prepersonal gods of unconscious emotions, moods, and complexes, deifying them with names borrowed from mythology. Some of us try to discard the notion of God altogether only to find our unlived spiritual drive inflating our political convictions to fantastic proportions. Some of us cast about in a jungle of meditative practices, astrology, health food, jogging. We say we are going inward, but find ourselves instead still in the prison of narcissism.

Many new movements in theology reach toward the missing concreteness of human presence coupled to the divine. Too much modern theology stresses the correlation of human and divine through abstract, rational concepts, emphasizing being as essence or existence. Now we are searching for how to find our being in the presence of Being, to find God's presence in the midst of human presence. Liberation theology centers on our political being, on the relation of God to economically and politically oppressed persons. Black theology finds God in the midst of racial oppression. Feminist theology finds God in the midst of sexual discrimination. All these theologies focus on the pains of concrete persons as central sources of insight into God's presence among us. Women offer unmistakably authoritative leadership here. If we receive into consciousness the feminine elements of being heretofore projected upon us, we can expect to see major social and theological changes as a result.

WOMEN AND PAIN: MINISTRY TO THE OUTCAST

What can specific women bring into our collective awareness? Above all, they can bring their sharp consciousness of pain—and the ministry that grows out of that. In every human experience— as reflected in Scripture, in literature, in so much of our lives— women have had the closest possible association with pain. Women have been denied jobs, not because they are unqualified, but merely because of their sex. They know firsthand what it is like to be flattened into a collective image and not seen as concrete persons. They know what it feels like to be met as both personal and nonpersonal, as individuals and as a type. Women bring a positive presence to pain because they know firsthand the experience of being pushed aside, skipped over, seen as sex objects or goddesses but not seen at all in their own concrete reality.

When one is canceled out in this way as a particular human being, one is left with a blank in the tissue of one's consciousness, a numb place, an agonizing wound. Through this break the unconscious comes rushing in, flooding us, because we have no interceding ego to shore up our aching inside against the battering from outside.[1] Women who learn to deal creatively with this sort of dehumanizing pain have a ministry to all people who suffer today in this way from others' projections. The "black," the "white," the "oppressor," the "oppressed," the "sexist"—these labels we project on each other obscure our humanness and bring with them every kind of pain.

How do we deal with the pain? By turning toward this wounding, by accepting it and developing a personal feeling toward it, we use it and overcome it rather than let it overcome us. We must feel the bruises all the way down, and not simply accumulate unconscious, undigested hurt feelings, with which we cannot and do not deal. Accumulated grievances build a shell of defensiveness around us. They tempt us to do to others what they have done to us, making them into nonpersons just as they have done with us.

To be present to this pain, to receive this hurt inwardly, is to achieve a deeply reconciling experience. Gathering this pain, which has fallen into the unconscious, back into consciousness and suffering it, is the only sure way to end it. The great blessing of finitude is that things do come to an end. Receiving and consciously feeling the hurt done them is one way that women can bring the force of their caring into the world.

Women's openness to pain deeply affects their use of negative aggression. All of us are able to express aggression more freely when we are not brought down by an undertow of complaints, reproaches, and other manifestations of undigested hurt. We are less apt to use a present issue to vent our rage at a past enemy. In this way we can direct our aggression against life-destroying structures and mass-mindedness, and can do so cleanly, with strong blows.

When we have touched the outcast pain in ourselves, and not projected it onto someone else, we are touching the outcast in others. We are receptive to what others may not yet be receiving in themselves. Feeling our pain, we can speak to the unconscious pain in others. Thus we develop a ministry to the spiritually impoverished, those rich or poor among us who have been left out of awareness, who have not been attended to, and who as a result have not received great chunks of themselves. We embark on a ministry of grace, going out to seek what has been overlooked or lost—like the woman and the lost coin of Scripture. If even one kind of concrete person is overlooked, then the position we hold is the wrong position.

With a clear opening to pain, we may be able to move through some of our anger to the grace of forgiveness, to receive in ourselves what has so often been rejected in us by others. We go into the pain and receive it. We stop attacking everybody because of the pain. We go into it, speak out of it, move through it. This brings into play in our life an unsentimental compassion. We are kept from despair over the cruelty we blindly do each other. By not reacting with a *quid pro quo*, but rather accepting the suffering instead, we allow our pain to come into receptive awareness. We work through and finish it there, creating an enabling space into which others may receive their cast-out feelings back into consciousness. This kind of toughness creates an echoing softness of atmosphere where things may grow, where a life of quality for women may be possible—and through women for men.

WOMEN AND THE BODY

A major projection that almost always falls onto women, even in these enlightened times, is everything connected with the body. Woman is thought to stand for sex and mortality. Her body, from which we all are born, is taken as a symbol of life and of death, of human mortality in all its aspects. In more abstract terms, woman is thought to represent our existence and its material base. She is what matters.

Many people never really face mortality, never really live in the sense of consciously realizing and facing what is actually happening to them. They exist instead from one experience to the next, with little or no consciousness. They exist as if in a dream. They are somewhere else, in a fantasy world, waiting for an imagined future, sadly mulling a troubled and an all too disposable past. They are nowhere touched by what is real now. Jung sums up the dangers in avoiding life in the here and now: "The more one has lived outside of life, the more one tries to defend oneself against it and invents all sorts of security mechanisms such as Adler describes so aptly . . . , the fictions by which one makes oneself safe. It is always safety against life, safety against the here and now, instead of submitting to things as they are. With the attitude of the here and now, you make the best of a situation, you say what you have to say, and do what you have to do."[2]

The woman who receives the projection of the body and does not identify with it but lifts it into consciousness helps others to live in the here and now. Hers is a remarkably positive ethic, a personal response that conveys a strong value judgment about what is happening to her. She is insisting on her particular point of view, telling us how a matter appears to her in the concrete reality of her life. Issues change this way. No event has its inevitable outcome in the presence of such a woman.

A woman who elects consciousness must fight almost indomitable sexual projections, her own and others'. There is the fear of many women, for example, that their body instincts, desires, needs, and emotions will rise up to overwhelm them if they allow them too much freedom. Women also carry the projection of the body's mortality, and the dread that death stirs in us. Otto Rank finds that the fear of mortality lies at the heart of the discrimination against woman because it is she who gives birth. That fact reminds us painfully that our life is finite, that we grow old and die, in spite of all our fantasies to the contrary. We come from the flesh and perish with the flesh. Women have long been saddled with this fear of the flesh that decays, that dies, that proclaims the death of all of us.

At this point, we catch a glimpse of a genuinely new opportunity for women and therefore for all of us, a new way to react to this phenomenon of projection. We can receive it but not become it. We must not identify with projections and yet equally we must not repress them from consciousness either. Precisely because we are the objects of so many projections, we must come to deal with them. We need neither angrily repudiate the projections, nor try to talk people out of them, nor identify with what is projected upon us. Instead we can see the images projected; we can stand aside from them and return them to the persons projecting them.

We can say openly such things as: "Look, this image is in the air between us; this is what you are projecting onto me. What do we make of this now? What is this all about? What is it about me that draws this projection? What is this image that you should be receiving yourself that you insist belongs to me?"

This action of receiving a projection enlarges the consciousness of both projector and projectee, making consciousness wider, fuller, deeper. Women doing this can mediate to all of us awareness of unconscious projected contents. Receiving them, we can work on integrating them and openly and positively use the contents so long associated with the feminine mode of being human.

By mediating to people's consciousness their projections of the body onto women, women can enlarge and make accessible the meanings associated with the body. In the church, for example, we have the body of the laity. In depth psychology there is the body of experience we call the unconscious, that matrix out of which our experience grows, with all the mental processes that flow beneath the surface of consciousness, the river of being from which our consciousness takes its life-giving water.[3] Woman is indelibly associated with the unconscious and its preverbal, nonrational images. To bring awareness of these unconscious images helps us all to be more sensitive to what the philosopher Karl Popper calls our "world of expectations."[4] These are not immutable, *a priori*, set contents. Our experiences may in fact prove them wrong, or mysterious and beyond full understanding. But, as Popper argues, we bring into life at birth certain strong expectations and from our conscious interaction with them develop what he calls "World Three," the domain of cultural forms and human values, of civilization. Like Mary's action in Scripture, we need to receive into consciousness images of the expectations that inhabit us, to ponder them, interact with them, and await what new insight into truth may take shape in the body of our individual and collective experience.

Like Mary, we need to seize with bold authority the presence of truth the unconscious delivers to us.

The witch in fairy tales serves as an example of one such image. She beautifully compensates for our strong conscious emphasis on the feminine as a motherly figure who always feeds us and gives herself ceaselessly to others. The witch does not feed others, but takes others to feed herself. She does not give sweets to children, but lures them into her cookie house so the children can sweeten her. A remote, alien figure, always in the deepest part of the forest, or at the farthest reach of the sea, she stands for the most remote aspects of human life, those outside human conventions and their attendant values. Devoid of human warmth, stripped of concern for others' feelings, she brings with her the breath of the uncanny. It is as if in seeing her we were looking straight at the awfulness of being. Receiving a witch image into consciousness and pondering its impact, a woman may find a new balance between her urge to give herself to others and her need to pursue her own goals. Receiving this witch image into our collective cultural images of the female can rectify our unbalanced views of woman as merely supporter and helpmate. It points to her canny intelligence, her capacity to exercise power, her great logic of the emotions. These could contribute so much to the life of the community if allowed full expression.[5]

The emphasis on the body and its association with females has something to do, I think, with the increased discussion and openness about lesbianism. Looked at symbolically, we may understand lesbianism as a doubling up of women to underline and support the feminine that has so long been neglected. The danger lies in the temptation to do to men what we feel men have done to women to exclude them. Lesbianism may be mixed with long repressed feelings of scorn, hostility, and hatred of men.

WOMEN AND THE LIFE OF PARADOX

The female stands forth as a bearer of an extraordinary paradox, the paradox of the simultaneity of personal and nonpersonal life, the paradox of the mixture of the concrete and the symbolic. Women are emerging now from the stereotypes and collective labels fixed on them. We are learning to improvise our own particular identities out of all our elements, of body, culture, and psyche, of our individual gifts, and of our limits. We stand for new ways of dealing with projections. We are working to bring sexual images into consciousness, not simply identifying with projected images, or angrily repudiating them. What have been warring opposites of the masculine and feminine need no longer blur into an undifferentiated unity or simply be ignored. We can arrive at the other side. Bit by bit we can integrate these opposites in ourselves and others, creating a new concreteness of real flesh-and-blood persons living in space and time, more fully themselves than they have been before. To push beyond the polarization of the sexes is possible only in a step-by-step process, effected by particular persons with concrete identities openly worn. It cannot be achieved by fiat. A receiving woman knows a special ministry to the particularity of persons, against abstract definitions and prescriptive stereotypes. She probes being in its many concrete, individual faces. Through her reception of differences between the sexes, she makes perceptible the similarity of the sexes. She knows that to focus on concrete persons does not lead to a confining personalism. The personalist way is a false way; it issues from the artificial compartmentalization of persons into public and private spheres, the inevitable sterility bred by people in categorical confinement. To focus on persons rather than categories is to reopen the flow of life, to see persons gathered in communities rather than collectives, into intimacies with each other rather than statistical units, person next to person all around the world.

Symbolically, a receiving woman is prefigured in the religious event of Mary's assumption into heaven bodily. Mary, a virgin, and Elizabeth, a barren woman, were not especially good choices for their time, when to be chosen meant to be loved and able to give love. In a male-dominated society the Gospel story focuses on women and the role their children will have. In the dogma of her Assumption, Mary brings into God's presence the human presence, that of a particular, concrete, embodied person. Receiving easily and openly all that came to her particular self, she stands forth in dogma as an archetypal receiver of other particular selves. She gives image to a singular new consciousness that neither chooses between opposites nor avoids them, but instead reaches across to encompass them.

The receiving woman who can give abundant particularity to new realizations of ancient images is the missing element in our society. Nothing in our liturgy, as yet, deals adequately with such a being present to oneself in the presence of God as Mary offers, such a receiving of oneself, a voting of faith in human presence in the universe because God has voted faith in us first. Simple reductions will not do; now we must enlarge human presence, step by step, detail by detail. As long ago as the fourteenth century, the mystic Dame Julian of Norwich invoked the presence of the Mother Jesus, and in her the Motherhood of God, not as a cause, not as a doctrinal problem, not as a theological definition, but as a matter of presence.[6]

JUDEO-CHRISTIAN RELIGION
AND THE FEMALE ELEMENT OF BEING

When Christian faith acts in a liberating way on women, it does so because it holds to its own center of being and directs women to focus on their own center of being. When traditional faith veers off into false-doing, it violates the life of people and exerts a constricting, antilife effect, particularly upon women.

We all begin in a vulnerable, dependent state, where everything depends on our mothers. Fear of this vulnerability and dependence makes us flee into false-doing, into hatred of the female, and into attitudes of almost compulsive alienation where love is replaced by hate. Christian faith offers us the refuge and resource to face this fear and to learn from the ancient truth that a mighty God can be found in precisely this vulnerable state. His own incarnate life began when he was born of a woman, dependent on her, his mother, to reflect back to him a sense of his own being. Those of us deprived as children of this loving response to our being may find it in the richly nurturing images of our religious tradition. We can discover there the God who seeks us where we must be found, in the flesh of our vulnerability.

Our earliest experiences with our mothers lay the groundwork for our human identity, both individually and as members of a group. That fact of life must be faced in all its starkness and all its implications. In recent years, we have avoided it, downplayed it, even challenged it outright in order not to back ourselves into a corner where women could be further abused. Either their faulty mothering has been blamed for all the problems of their offspring, or their motherhood has been deified to ridiculous and distorted heights. Both attitudes prevent the ordinary mother from finding her own rhythms as a parent because she has been made to feel she must attain some sort of impossible perfection. In addition, fathers have again and again been totally forgotten, both for praise or blame, as if they had nothing whatever to do with newborn children after the initial conception. As a last indignity, the woman who chooses not to bear children has been condemned and ostracized as "unfeminine."

These distortions offer classic examples of the fatal error of reifying and then projecting psychological insights. As a result we both distort the insights and lose access to the wide range of women's personalities. Insight then turns into prescription or proscription. We can heartily sympathize with the arguments directed at throwing out such insights altogether if they can only lead to stereotyped norms to be imposed on the lives of women. Nonetheless the insight is profound and inescapable. The foundation of our capacity to live from the core of our own being is in this first mother-infant relationship. To receive this fact into consciousness is to see new possibilities. Foremost among them is a new way to style mothering. How can society legally and culturally support its women in their *own* sense of being? How can society help them to be themselves, living out of their own core of being, without guilt, so that if they choose to have a baby they can better receive and respond to their child's own special being? A radical social change results from this sequence of receiving. Our work patterns undergo a revolution.

I have argued for years that when women are admitted to jobs that heretofore only men have filled, they must not be expected to do the job in the same old way. If we hire a nursing mother, for example, we must not expect her to sit through four-hour committee meetings. We may need to style the committee meetings differently—with great benefit to everyone. As any veteran of such gatherings knows, the length of meetings is never commensurate with the volume of work turned out. On the contrary—the shorter the meeting, the more is accomplished. Men, too, would begin to see that they can shape their work more flexibly according to individual temperaments and gifts. We would do more work that way and give it greater spirit and meaning.

A principle emerges. Society must support the being of women while women support the being of their infants. Constrictive work schedules and restrictive job concepts must be changed to meet the nature of both women and men, not simply of one sex. This principled answer to ancient and modern problems of changing the job is simple in comparison with all those futile efforts to try to change persons.

We may well wonder why, if the answer is so simple, it has not been accepted long before now. It seems incredible that we would try to change woman's nature rather than rearrange schedules to accommodate her as she is. It seems equally mad that society should have tried to turn over children en masse to impersonal agencies, casting aside the unduplicatable connection between mother and infant as if it were a minor element in their lives and not the very essence of them.[7] We insist that the dilemma of career or motherhood is insoluble, as if it were women's problem alone, and did not belong to men and women, and did not have to be solved for the health of our society as a whole.

We need to change work schedules to permit women employees to become fully involved with their babies without the threat of losing pay or advancement in their careers. Instead of an inflexible nine-to-five workday in the office, we must introduce variety in women's work hours as well as in the location of their jobs. Some work can be done at home. Some can be done at night. In this way a society can recognize that its children depend on their parents to nurture their being. In this way a society will accept openly the truth that built into the responsibilities of work is the job of parenting, and parenting applies to both fathers and mothers. Thus we can relieve woman, who for so long has carried the impossible burden of guilt when she neglects her child to work and of fear when she neglects her work to be with her child.

We can banish the conditions that breed guilt and fear much more easily than we can repair the damaged core of a child's being for which our society is paying staggering tolls in custodial, penal, and therapeutic services. Obviously, society benefits directly from supporting the growth of citizens who feel alive and free from the false- or forced-doing that begets crime as a way of acquiring power to make up for lack of identity. Society loses when workers suffer every kind of illness, mental and physical, as outward signs of inward loss of being.

A change of work hours to flexible schedules, responsive to workers' actual lives and sexual identities, invariably must enlarge the being of working persons, making being rather than productivity the central concern. Surprisingly enough, the quality and output of work will improve as a result. But this must make sense on its own human terms to any thoughtful person. When a work schedule itself nurtures the being of workers, work must become more like play. The few examples I know of where this has been tried prove its success.[8]

Reception of the full significance of female elements of being leads to a new style of parenting. It emphasizes a parent's quality of presence to a child, rather than the quantity of time spent in proximity to the child. Being there in a receptive way calls for presence and response more than for action and accomplishment. This sort of presence in a mother—or father—involves active attentiveness but neither intrusion on a parent's part nor withdrawal. A fully present mother remains open to her child and the opportunity of the moment. She spends time playing with her child rather than merely tolerating the child while she concentrates on her daily tasks. A short spell of this sort of presence supports a child's being far more than constant physical nearness while she is psychologically preoccupied with other concerns.

Every mother knows the vast difference between these two kinds of presence. In one she is really with her child, touched at the core of her being as she touches her child's. In the other she exists separately, only tangentially accepting the company of her child while her central attention focuses on something else. The first sort of presence receives and promotes the child's own sense of self-proclamation, as in one way or another it says, "I am, I am here, I count." It paves the way for every kind of future capacity to mingle self with other selves, with ideas, with ecstasy. The other way conveys a sense of being outside things, perhaps politely and tolerantly, but still excluded. The child feels it has not been fully recognized and received; it is not altogether present and may never be. In one, a person comes into being, in its own fragile, unique reality, its value beyond price. In the other, a shell, a make-believe person, is devised, in order to assure survival.

For women in particular, receiving is symbolized in attentiveness to the emerging being of a child, though it by no means confines itself to that. With a child we are more apt to persist in such receiving and to muster the necessary energy to sustain it over long periods of time, because a child gives such direct response to our efforts. A child wails when we become preoccupied, yells when we shut off our attention, smiles at our good humor, coos over our caresses, and simply expands into its own self under our beneficent care. Our child's response to our efforts encourages us.

We ourselves need this same sort of open, alert attentiveness to our female being to bring into existence our own contributions—in scholarship, in the arts, in business, in love relationships, in all the strenuous encounters of human experience. Usually, we cannot muster the energy for these sorts of births and rebirths. We find it easy to dodge them in the duties of our constricted lives. We fail to nourish them because they cannot encourage us with quite the same directness that a child can, wilting or blooming before us. Also in a curious way we discover that we of all people are dependent on our children—both actually and symbolically. We need our children to reflect back to us our own coming-into-being, in just the way our children depend on us. Our businesses, our works of art, our professional undertakings—inanimate as they so often must be—cannot reflect back to us so directly who we are.

Women are constantly reminded physically of the necessity to receive being. Our very anatomy is built around a place of openness. Psychologically, our symbolic and cultural traditions emphasize our need and desire to be opened up and supported by another in love.

Part of the mystery of woman's appeal is her receptive openness, the availability and responsiveness that spring from her physical and psychological being. In becoming aware of their being, women become aware of their vulnerability to existence itself. For this openness spells great danger—women may be violated, forcefully invaded, or left open with no one to receive. Women may be left uncompleted, unfulfilled, doomed to live unseen and unreceived. Their vulnerability leaves them open to deep hurt.

One of the central tasks for a woman is to learn how to accept her openness without being hurt beyond repair, to discover an articulate anger with which to defend against further pain. Women need to learn how to permit vulnerability without covering over their openness with a hard crust of defensive opinionizing. They need to become aggressive to be tough enough to survive, and yet to survive with all their own feeling intact.

A DIFFERENT KIND OF KNOWING

Receiving into consciousness the knowing that comes through being-one-with, without falling into identification with that mode of knowing, ushers in new theological possibilities. Enough psychological research has been done to accept as valid this mode of knowing by identification with what one knows. The problem lies in how to receive this fact. As we saw in Chapter 2, this fearful mode of apprehension is all too easily projected onto women in an effort to control it. Or it is rejected outright, simply annihilated from consciousness. Or people identify with it, which is another way of trying to avoid it. To receive this way of knowing as one epistemological option affects our religious life directly.

Many women feel intense anger at the church and the Judeo-Christian tradition for what they feel is a refusal to see them as women. Women have suffered exclusion from priestly office. Religious language and imagery stress the masculine even when the rhetoric is highly metaphorical. Stress on Mary as gentle and meek excludes her fierce aggression and monumental power to endure. Women's anger can be seen now as a sign of their determination to move out of this unseen position. They make a loud declaration that says "I am!" or "We are!"

Women now have a great opportunity to throw off what Melanie Klein calls projective identification, where women have been identified with the mode of knowing-by-identifying that has been projected upon them.[9] We must do this, however, without losing access to the reality that this way of knowing encompasses. Our anger must mobilize our aggression to hold in consciousness simultaneously the opposites of perceiving reality as objectively separate from ourselves, and of making subjective identification with it. We need neither fear the identification nor equate ourselves with only this one mode of knowing.

Temptations to avoid this task take several forms. First, fearful of this feminine way of knowing, we reject it bitterly. We develop a cold resistance to any emphasis on the feminine modes as well as to actual women who seek ordination. As we saw in Chapter 2,[10] this fear of the feminine capacity, in men as well as women, is managed by projecting the capacity onto women and trying to keep them "in their place."

No better is the opposite temptation,[11] to indulge our anger and identify with it in the face of prejudiced and unjust treatment of women. It is much easier to set oneself against familiar stereotypes than to develop new attitudes. For developing the new means time-consuming labor, which will tax our imaginations and aggressive energies to the fullest. The negative mode—simply declaring oneself against something—quickly gives one the illusion of a clear sense of identity, if nothing else an unmistakable difference from the "enemy." But in our rage against an adversary, in our rejection of that "other" and our declaration of independence from "them," we hide our actual continuing dependence on them to serve as defining points for what we *are* by marking off what we *are not*. Thus some women are tempted to reject males and the masculine altogether, excluding men as they have felt excluded by men, thereby betraying their dependency on what they reject as part of their self-definition—the masculine. Almost always they end up by imitating its most hostile and rejecting ways. In the church this imitative attitude leads to a separatist movement of so-called "post-Christian feminist spirituality," where a feminist identity supersedes one's identity as a child of God. Psychologically, the roots of this separatism arise from persons falling into unconscious identity with the mode of knowing by being-one-with, then reifying it and prescribing it as the only way to be. A person's fanatic embrace of the mode of being-one-with may appear as acceptance of it, but that is a sham, quickly evidenced by that person's compulsive insistence that it is the only true way of knowing. Then the familiar us-them mentality follows, with the projection of all evil onto anyone who holds different views.

A third temptation (the third detour of Chapter 2)[12] is to throw out both the masculine and feminine modalities of being and knowing in favor of a unisexual androgyne. This alternative presents the danger of regression to a presexual, disembodied, ethereal identity, where the whole issue of sexual differentiation has not yet emerged into awareness and is not allowed to do so. Instead of integrating two modalities of being into a fresh and unique personality of man or woman, we lose the clear definition of either to a blurry indefiniteness that masquerades as man-woman. That sort of identity differs significantly from the strong male who possesses large feminine sensibilities, or the vibrant female who manifests vigorous masculine qualities. The men and women who possess their contrasexual sides confidently and clearly stand out from the shapeless unisexual as flexible and open, large in their identities as men or women. In contrast, the androgyne exudes an indefiniteness that on closer inspection often turns out to be an as yet uprooted identity that cannot endure the stresses of sexual commitment. In psychological terms we are talking about the difference between a pre-Oedipal and a post-Oedipal personality.

The pre-Oedipal person is not yet formed in his or her own identity, does not yet possess a rudimentary core of superego conscience, for that is one of the legacies bequeathed to us by working through Oedipal conflict. Thus the religious feeling associated with unisex identity tends to regress to premonotheistic phases of religious formation. There, one is apt to identify as religious any intense or startling experience of incipient identity of self, whether through an unconscious dream, a spontaneous image, or a special moment with another person, to the exclusion of the ethical, the prophetic, or the transcendent aspects of faith where one feels addressed and even commanded. Of special importance is the experience of ambivalence that is so marked in pre-Oedipal life—those emotions of love and hate, good and bad, both in oneself and others. The image of God associated with such experience of ambivalence is apt to include a notion of God's having an "evil" or "dark" side. These pre-Oedipal levels are not to be slighted nor are they to be discarded when we reach religious maturity. But they are not the whole story either. If these parts are taken for the whole, a kind of exacerbated immanentism may result, or even worse, a form of idolatry where we deify natural, and particularly psychic, processes.

To say we must include both modalities of being human, however, means going to the most concrete levels, connecting our faith to God's presence in us and to us. All the false crosses people have been taking up—acting toward men, toward women, or toward sexual differentiation as if these were the enemy—are pseudo solutions. On close inspection such solutions reveal themselves as schemes of hate directed against the female elements of being. They evade the real issue: our need to receive all of our being. False-doing that seeks to replace the feminine with the masculine or the masculine with the feminine has at last come to be recognized. To abolish all notions of sexual difference now in favor of androgyne is once again to ignore the female in herself, in her many kinds of self. The feminine is not an indistinct part of an androgynous whole. Rather, it brings necessary rectification to a serious sexual imbalance by adding to consciousness our major missing part.

Knowing through the mode of being-one-with means having at conscious disposal a mode of identifying in which we know that we know this way. It means being greatly conscious of our subjectivity, as well as recognizing that we know through differentiation, separating ourselves from the object known. To know about this identifying mode means we need no longer see it only as a way to be outgrown and left behind with the vulnerabilities of childhood or the infant's frightening helplessness.

We must not seize upon this mode as the single style of operation, however. We must stretch to receive for conscious disposal all ways of knowing and being, developing a receptiveness that permits a counterpoint between the two main forms, thus enlarging our capacity to respond to others. A woman with firm access to her own animus gains a means of understanding men from the inside out, so she can see things at a point closer to a man's point of view, even when it strongly conflicts with her own. She knows more latitude, both in identifying with another's view and in holding firmly to her own. Her response is therefore richer, subtler, more receptive to the complexities of existence. It is no longer a simpleminded us-them reduction.

A woman's capacity to be one with the immediate concrete being before her, whether person, idea, or creative impulse, does not necessarily reduce her capacity for perspective, to see the long-range view, to grasp the abstract norm of truth. This permits no easy return to total subjectivity. Her larger consciousness holds both subjective knowing *with* and objective knowing *about* the other in contrapuntal rhythm. Thus consciousness no longer becomes the end-all of the process in a kind of modern idolatry, the sort of blind knowing that extracts valuable ore from the land but damages the environment for generations. It is not the detached all-knowingness that provokes a schizoid condition where one feels alive only in one's head, with only one's own mental processes seeming real. It is not the statistical kind of knowing that affects an objectivity verging on inhumanity. And it certainly is not the psychotic extreme torn away from any being-one-with, where one can consent to individual murder or genocide.

THEOLOGY CHANGES

Experience of contrapuntal styles of knowing issues in an entirely different kind of doing. Theology informed by knowing as being-one-with cannot and will not indulge in the simplistic reductions of social engineering, infusing the Godhead with the latest cultural fads. In the last decades, God has been said to be dead, black, red, and female. Theology may resume its core task of articulating in words and images our profound preverbal and pre-Oedipal experience of God's being-one-with us, and our post-Oedipal experience of God's continuing-to-be. This experience of reality will abundantly supply our efforts to describe it.

To take but one example—the immanence and transcendence of God are categories that traditionally have been sharply opposed. An immanent mother-god is replaced by a transcendent Yahweh, standing above human experience, not to be identified with any human attribute, a distant patriarch overseeing all. For many, however, the distance becomes too great, so that contact with God is all but abolished. Regression to the original formulation of a God identified with natural forces solves nothing—even when those forces include our psyches, so that self-actualization or individuation assumes godlike proportions. This process starts an alternation of opposites all over again.

To experience God's being-at-one-with us and atoning action, aided by our own capacity to know through identifying, leads to a mingling of the categories of the transcendent and the immanent. The result is a more complete image of God's being as a presence that is both powerful and vulnerable. We discover the falsity of the old polarization of transcendent–immanent: in fact, they are two ways we experience God's otherness. The author of being seeks us at the core of our being, pulling us into all we can be, summoning us with this incalculable largeness that altogether effaces our little categories, our notions of what kind of spirituality we need, what kinds of sexual roles we should play and prescribe for others. The Holy "I am who I am" summons us with a blunt command: "Be who you are. Be all that you are."

What does this mean in human terms? Close inspection of female figures in Scripture gives good examples. Two Marys demonstrate an immediate and lavish response to Jesus, in which they cut across all the usual boundaries we erect between sexuality and spirituality, receptivity and aggression, the human and the divine. One woman weeps on Jesus' feet and dries them with her hair. Another woman buys costly ointment to anoint Jesus' head. Both women pour their love upon God—a passionate, sexual, and spiritual response—neither a blind nor a narcissistic emotion, but one that is alert in its perception of who Jesus is. These women know something about this great holy figure that others do not. One Mary knows Jesus' forgiveness of her sins, out of a love that cannot be earned by rule-keeping good conduct. The other Mary knows intuitively the death and suffering that are soon to befall Jesus. In a boldly aggressive act of love she leaves behind her those categories that still restrain us today as they did the disciples then. The disciples asked, with unmistakable skepticism, what good was her devotion? She should be spending that money on the poor.

Again, we fail to see what that wise woman saw through her penetrating knowing, a knowing that was in fact a being-at-one-with, a fact that Jesus saw and marked for all eternity as the central power not only of her faith but of faith itself. She alone ministered to him who came to minister to us. She alone acted as servant to the servant of man.

These women and the other women at the foot of the cross were not officially designated apostles. Yet they alone had the distinction of not betraying Jesus or deserting him at the end. Their way of knowing and loving him, so deeply receptive, to the point of identifying with his presence, was a gathering of aggression to endure without turning away—past disappointment, past disillusionment, past death—to the end of his suffering. The other Mary, Magdalene, offers an example of the astounding "doing" that springs up naturally from her knowing of Jesus at the core of her being. She alone acts as apostle to the apostles, proclaiming to them the stunning news of the resurrection. The feminine way of being and knowing brings with it an astonishing range of perception and response. Different aspects of the life and work of faith come boldly forward this way. We need these, not to deify them as the only ways of faith, but to take nourishment from them by the great accrual of being they bring.

A secure sense of our ongoing being that moves directly into the world has unexpected implications for Christian faith. The interruption of personal continuity of being leads to false-doing, pursued in order to cope with the unbearable suffering that comes from lack of being a person at the core. Persons afflicted with psychotic disorder show us stark examples of this sort of suffering. Persons rigid with a catatonic fixity, persons grossly dissociated from their bodies as shown in smearing their rooms with feces or their compulsive fingering of their genitals in public, persons shouting in fear at persecutory voices only they hear—all such persons shock us with their pain. Yet our own more ordinary suffering displays the same acutely painful sources: gaps in our core of being; an inability to show by being one with what we know; constant interruptions of our sense of being. Where there should be a theme of continuous being, dead air spaces instead interrupt and invade us. Where there should be a whole fabric of being, holes appear like lost stitches. Where there should be a firm foundation of being to stand upon, cracks and fissures appear and we fall through.

This lack of being—whether large or small—comprises what Christian doctrine describes as evil: the privation of being. This is that evil which is the absence of being. Where we are led into temptation and not delivered from evil, where we cooperate with it, evil becomes sin. To the lack that is already there we add the lack we create by our deliberate absence from the being we possess. We turn away from the being we possess and add to old gaps new, self-made ones, widening them, focusing on the lost spaces only. We disregard the larger fabric that holds the holes, widening the cracks by poking into them instead of resting on the firm foundation that surrounds those fissures. We extend the dead air space instead of building up the solidity in us.

Into these empty gaps rush our negative emotions and dreads, our resentments, grudges, vengeance, envies, hatreds, and lusts for total control. From these sources spring our myriad false-doings, manufactured to cover over the holes in our being.

In old-fashioned religious language, the devil (all the negative forces that possess us) grabs us in the places where the gaps show our weaknesses. There our souls are stolen. There we lose our uniqueness. The disease that arises from this loss of the core of our self, the ontological insecurity in which we then live, lays us open to all the powers of evil. We cannot imagine a continuity of being. We grab at being to possess it and thus are unable to take it when it is offered to us. Our activities become frantic and are aptly characterized in classical language as the sins of greed, envy, anger.

We develop an outsized lust for things, for sex, for power. We revel in our slothful refusal to be who we are. All these terrors germinate in the dark cavities of our being, those great yawning empty holes. We will do anything rather than face them, even if it means bringing down the house of being upon our heads.

How, we might ask, can these terrible fissures exist? How do they come about? How can God permit persons to live with such gaps in their being? Why are we made so frighteningly dependent on each other, that we can hurt each other so fatefully?

Traditional meditations on the problem of evil formulate it in *either/or* conceptual terms. Either there is an all-good God who is not all powerful, or an all-powerful God who is not all good. But the classical ways of reconciling an all-good and all-knowing God with an omnipotent being who permits evil are emotionally inaccessible to many people today. Accepting the female element of being and going all the way back to its source yields a way out of this critical difficulty. Dame Julian of Norwich provides its central argument: God creates all good and suffers all evil.[13] That is the way we evaluate our decisions and our actions. Do they build up being or do they tear it down? We cease to focus on the abstract question of why evil exists. We turn instead to the concrete existential issue of how to bear the searing vulnerability of being, facing head on that it is more important to receive being than to do anything else. If we do, we may yield less to temptations to run from the gaps in our being by escapisms into false-doing, and come closer to accepting ourselves, with joy and with ease.

God suffers all evil. Even there, in the gaps of our own being, God is one with us. God in Jesus takes on our sins. Being is vulnerable at its divine core to the most radical of human failures. We may take heart, then, when we try to suffer awareness of the gaps in our own being, when we try to receive and not repress, to receive and not fall into identity with those personalized and social gaps where false-doing and pseudo-heroic solutions breed hate, where hardness of heart is our only defense against vulnerability of being. We may take heart because we are admitted, gaps and all, into the heart of being.

We may see a way to bring to those gaps in ourselves, those places of broken-off being, a feminine way of knowing. We must learn to be with ourselves just as God in the crucifixion is with us. We must see a way to receive into awareness our gaps, a way that neither represses them altogether nor falls into a state of identity with them. Repressing them leads to false-doing. Falling into the gaps leads only to an imprisoning narcissism or to madness. Leaning on God who creates good and suffers evil is something else entirely. It means holding in continuous awareness the gaps that occur in our being. This way goodness comes out of evil, for our awareness extends our continuity of being onto the other side of the gaps, around the gaps, holding them, receiving them in a persistent line like a necklace alternating knots and pearls. We grow around our wounds and come to be able to sustain them in the larger central sequences of our lives.

THE HIDDENNESS OF REVELATION

Our ability to do all of this comes from our learning how to receive our being in the feminine way, at the wounded core. It comes from our acknowledging our dependency on being-one-with others. It springs from the knowledge that this has already been accomplished for us by God. Held in the amplitude of grace, as on a mother's lap, we see not just who we are and are able to be, but also who we are not able to be, where we are hidden, interrupted, and broken. Receiving being means accepting vulnerability, even if we are terribly afraid; it means knowing-with-others, even if it brings pain; it means going on being despite all the gaps and violations of our being. Such fear and pain and suffering form the cross of being human. But a tough-minded receiving carries its own staying power, for we see then that God stays with us and extends the comprehensive power of the resurrection into a joyous celebration of being human.

Receiving being means a different kind of revelation of ourselves and of God. It is always revelation in the flesh, in the hidden spaces of the body of life. It is not crystal clear and immutable. It is not proclaimable as an abstract truth divorced from a context of living being. Neither is it reducible to one's own inner processes, or to one's mood or latest psychological insight or dream, or to one's socioeconomic situation or politics.

Receiving being points a way through the present barrenness of spirit aggravated by a theology cut off from its roots in God's presence, a theology turned to linguistic exercises, political exhortation, or evangelical moralizing. But the opposite tendency—to regress to a premonotheistic stage in the delusion that it comprises an advance to call natural processes of the psyche "momentary gods"[14]—is in fact to retreat from the tough realities of the world and it is not one bit better. Nor is it any improvement to inflate one's particular concept of justice or one's political bias into the whole story, in effect raising up another idol in place of the God one has lost.

Each alternative seizes one pole to the exclusion of the other and so exacerbates the polarization—between self and world, private and public, abstract and concrete, political and psychological, rational and nonrational, male gods and monotheism, female goddesses and polytheism. No, we need all of these parts of human experience and a consciousness large and receptive enough to hold them all.

Receiving our long-hidden revelation means there is no God to be found divorced from the flesh of our experience. We receive God in the vulnerability of our subjective bias, in our emotional and historical context, in our suffering. But we do not receive God when we elevate these parts into the whole. To receive the hidden

God is not to lay hold on a rigid definition. The more we see into the darkness of God's presence, the more darkness is revealed, for this God is a presence, alive and real, and not bottleable like a genie. This is a wounded God, not a formula. If we receive this God, we too must receive our wounds. But the God revealed in the flesh of experience is a God, not ourselves; an Other, not a projection of our psychic processes; an objective presence that comes *to* us, not a reification of subjective content that comes *out* of us. Being received by a God other than ourselves makes it possible for us to receive this hidden God into us. Thus emphasis on the flesh of immediate concrete life means neither loss of objective perspective nor being mired in total subjectivism. It means a rearrangement of those old mutually exclusive dichotomies of subjective and objective. What is "really true" does not necessarily exclude the "merely personal." What is personal does not exclude the larger overview that stretches to cover all people. God is presence not rules. God is alive and real and near. But God is God, not one of us. So we must penetrate to still more hidden recesses. The more we uncover, the more we discover to uncover.

Vulnerability and knowing through being-one-with and persistence-in-being take on added significance this way. If received openly, they open us to more vulnerability and more receiving. Like the saints, we may reach a state of being where our core of self is assailable at any time by the God of presence who is the present God. In that presence, prayer is less something done apart from daily tasks and more something conducted in a counterpoint to those tasks. We pray unceasingly in the company of a God hidden in the ordinary day's events. Our knowing-by-being-with reaches farther than we thought possible. It uncovers all the deeply buried spiritual ambitions in us, leading us to find out something about being by joining being, to receive into consciousness our deepest spiritual aspirations by becoming one with them. We discover we want to be with what matters most to us, with what gives life to any and all being. No longer satisfied with substitute sensations of being we pursue inspection of who we really are and who others really are in all their differences and samenesses to us.

In the radical femininity of self, a receiving consciousness reaches to include all the different parts of self, with none left out. We want the self that is there, present, not a fantasy perfect self, not a repudiated bad self, but the concrete real self as it is, and as much of it as we can hold on to. Like the woman receiving otherness through the being of her child, we learn to nurture our connection to otherness. Like the woman receiving animus contents we get tougher, more able to tolerate ambiguity and ambivalence without splitting and projecting and indulging in prejudice against others onto whom we have projected what we cannot receive as parts of ourselves. Like the woman opening herself to her lover, we come to be able to tolerate being in increasing doses, no longer hiding from any of the terror of being. Because we really are receiving being we see it as veiled and accept it as hidden and recognize the grace of being able to touch the untouchable and see the unseeable.

Notes

Chapter 1. RECEIVING WOMAN

1. Sigmund Freud, "Femininity," in *New Introductory Lectures on Psychoanalysis* (W. W. Norton & Co., 1965), p. 135.

2. Ann Belford Ulanov, *The Feminine in Jungian Psychology and in Christian Theology* (Northwestern University Press, 1971), see pp. 41–42, 254–255, 275, 336–339; Ann and Barry Ulanov, *Religion and the Unconscious* (Westminster Press, 1975), see pp. 150–155, 236–237.

3. I am indebted here to Barry Ulanov's lecture "Literature in a Woman's Image," given at a workshop on "Religion in a Woman's Life: Limiting or Liberating?" sponsored by Trinity College, Middlebury College, the University of Vermont, Hopkins Book Shop, and St. Paul's Cathedral, Burlington, Vt., April 15, 1978. References are to Anna Ahkmatova, "The Muse," and Zenaida Hippius, "What Is Sin?" in *Modern Russian Poetry*, ed. and tr. by Vladimir Markov and Merrill Sparks (Bobbs-Merrill Co., 1966), p. 279 and p. 67, respectively; Nadezhda Mandelstam, *Hope Against Hope: A Memoir*, tr. by Max Hayward (Atheneum Publishers, 1970); Gertrud von Le Fort, *The Song at the Scaffold*, tr. by Olga Marx (Doubleday & Co., Image Book, 1961).

4. Donald W. Winnicott, *The Maturational Processes and the Facilitating Environment* (International Universities Press, 1965), p. 99.

5. All case material, unless otherwise indicated, is taken from my work as a psychotherapist, with thanks to the persons who permitted me to use their material.

6. Elizabeth Gaskell, *Mary Barton* (E. P. Dutton & Co., Everyman's Library, 1969), p. 366; see also pp. 352–353, 359.

7. Elizabeth Gaskell, *North and South* (London: John Lehmann, 1951), p. 404; see also pp. 411, 98.

8. See Phyllis Trible, *God and the Rhetoric of Sexuality* (Fortress Press, 1978); see also her "Depatriarchalizing in Biblical Interpretation," *Journal of the American Academy of Religion,* March 1973; and "Two Women in a Man's World: A Reading of the Book of Ruth," *Soundings,* Fall 1976.

9. Reported in *The New York Times,* 1976. See also *Our Bodies, Ourselves* (Simon & Schuster, 1973); Irene Claremont de Castillejo, *Knowing Woman* (G. P. Putnam's Sons, 1973); and Margaret Mead, "Why Do We Speak of Woman's Intuition?" in *Anima,* Vol. 1, No. 2, 1975, all of which attempt to address the feminine experience on its own terms.

10. See Ann Belford Ulanov, *The Feminine,* pp. 175–176; see also Mary Esther Harding, *Woman's Mysteries* (London: Longmans, Green & Co., 1936), pp. 234–235, 241–243; see also, Penelope Shuttle and Peter Redgrove, *The Wise Wound* (Richard Marek Publishers, 1978).

Chapter 2. DETOURS TO DEAD ENDS

1. Some attention has been given this deep-seated fear of the female. See, for example, Otto Rank, "Feminine Psychology and Masculine Ideology," Ch. 7 in *Beyond Psychology* (Dover, 1941); Karen Horney, "The Dread of Woman," in *Feminine Psychology* (W. W. Norton & Co., 1967); Wolfgang Lederer, *The Fear of Women* (Grune & Stratton, 1968).

2. A poignant symptom of this loss of roots in feminine identity is the modern Western woman's struggle with overweight. For discussion of this, see Ann Belford Ulanov, "Fatness and the Female," *Psychological Perspectives,* Vol. 10, No. 1, 1979.

3. See Edith Weigert, "Conditions of Organized and Regressive Responses to Danger," in her *The Courage to Love* (Yale University Press, 1970), pp. 168–175.

4. Jung describes the political and group implications of a diminished ego-identity thus: "A dim consciousness is always inclined to form something like a sect, a small group within which there is complete identity; as soon as anyone has a thought that differs from the thoughts and feelings of the others there is trouble, an explosion. . . . [There] can only be small communities with complete *participation mystique* inside and complete hostility and emotionality outside." C. G. Jung, *The Visions Seminars* (Zurich: Spring Publications, 1976), Book 2, p. 373.

5. Harold F. Searles, *Collected Papers on Schizophrenia and Related Subjects* (International Universities Press, 1965), p. 226.

6. Ibid., p. 227.

7. Ibid., p. 234; see also p. 220.
8. See ibid., pp. 222–223.
9. Harry Stack Sullivan claims that "loneliness in itself is more terrible than anxiety." Failure to gain relationship to others damages the self's orientation to living. See Harry Stack Sullivan, *The Interpersonal Theory of Psychiatry* (W. W. Norton & Co., 1953), p. 262.
10. C. G. Jung, *Mysterium Coniunctionis,* Collected Works, Vol. 14, tr. by R. F. C. Hull (Bollingen Series, XX; Pantheon Books, 1963), p. 180.
11. Bryan Magee, *Karl Popper* (Viking Press, 1973), p. 23.

Chapter 3. RELOCATING THE ISSUE

1. References are to C. G. Jung, "Anima and Animus," in his *Two Essays on Analytical Psychology,* Collected Works, Vol. 7, tr. by R. F. C. Hull (Bollingen Series, XX; Pantheon Books, 1953), pp. 188–212. See also Ann Belford Ulanov, "Jung on Male and Female," in Ruth Tiffany Barnhouse and Urban T. Holmes III, *Christian Approaches to Sexuality* (Seabury Press, 1976), pp. 197–212; Harry Guntrip, *Schizoid Phenomena, Object-Relations and the Self* (International Universities Press, 1969), pp. 249ff.; Donald W. Winnicott, *Playing and Reality* (Basic Books, 1971), pp. 72–75, 80–84, 132–135; David Bakan, *The Duality of Human Existence* (Beacon Press, 1966), Ch. IV; N. Chodorow, "Family Structure and Feminine Personality," in Michelle Zimbalist Rosaldo and Louise Lamphere (eds.), *Woman, Culture, and Society* (Stanford University Press, 1974); Jean Baker Miller, *Toward a New Psychology of Women* (Beacon Press, 1976); Melanie Klein, *The Psycho-Analysis of Children,* tr. by Alix Strachey (Delacorte Press/Seymour Lawrence, 1975), Chs. 11 and 12.
2. I am indebted to D. W. Winnicott's article "The Use of an Object and Relating Through Identifications," in his *Playing and Reality.*
3. For extended discussion of this sort of consciousness, see Ann and Barry Ulanov, "Intercession," Ch. 11 in their *Religion and the Unconscious,* pp. 218–243.

Chapter 4. RECEIVING THE FEMININE ELEMENTS OF BEING

This chapter is based on a lecture that I originally delivered in April 1978 in Burlington, Vermont, on the subject of "Religion in a Woman's Life: Limiting or Liberating?" sponsored by Trinity College, Middlebury College, the University of Vermont, Hopkins Book Shop, and St. Paul's Cathedral.

1. See Donald W. Winnicott, "Primary Maternal Preoccupation," in *Through Paediatrics to Psycho-Analysis: Collected Papers* (Basic Books, 1975), pp. 300–306.

2. See Ernst Cassirer, *Language and Myth,* tr. by Susanne K. Langer (Dover Publications, [1946]), pp. 7–11; see C. G. Jung, "Lecture V" in *The Symbolic Life: Miscellaneous Writings,* Collected Works, Vol. 18, tr. by R. F. C. Hull (Bollingen Series, XX; Princeton University Press, 1976), pp. 135–182; see Magee, *Karl Popper,* pp. 56–59.

3. I am indebted to D. W. Winnicott's idea of transitional space; see his *Playing and Reality,* Chs. 1, 3, 4.

4. Ann Belford Ulanov, *The Feminine,* Chs. 8, 9, 10.

5. See Winnicott, *Playing and Reality,* Ch. 5; see also Guntrip, *Schizoid Phenomena, Object-Relations and the Self,* pp. 249ff.; and Winnicott, *The Maturational Processes and the Facilitating Environment,* Chs. 3, 4, 7.

6. David Holbrook, *Human Hope and the Death Instinct* (Pergamon Press, 1971), pp. 54, 238; see also Chs. 19, 22, 24.

7. Ibid., p. 259; see also Winnicott, *The Maturational Processes and the Facilitating Environment,* pp. 87–88.

8. Over the centuries changes in images of Christ reflect changes in the self-image of believers.

9. See Julian of Norwich, *The Revelations of Divine Love,* tr. by James Walsh (Harper & Row, 1961), p. 103.

10. Holbrook, *Human Hope and the Death Instinct,* p. 266.

11. See Winnicott, *The Maturational Processes and the Facilitating Environment,* pp. 52–54, 86.

12. See Guntrip, *Schizoid Phenomena, Object-Relations, and the Self,* pp. 250–251; see also Holbrook, *Human Hope and the Death Instinct,* p. 191.

13. See R. D. Laing, *The Politics of Experience* (Penguin Books, 1967), p. 46; see also pp. 11, 38. Laing's tone has softened, however, in his most recent publications. We may speculate that this stems from his happy second marriage and a different experience of woman and of children from within a warm, loving relationship. See R. D. Laing, *Conversations with Adam and Natasha* (Pantheon Books, 1977).

14. See Jacques Lacan, *The Language of the Self: The Function of Language in Psychoanalysis,* tr. by Anthony Wilden (Johns Hopkins Press, 1968), pp. 11–13, 135, 173, 178–179, 300.

15. David Holbrook challenges head on the inevitability of alienation as put forth in the thinking of Sartre and Laing. Instead, Holbrook argues, alienation of this sort is part of the schizoid malady that afflicts persons

inadequately seen, focused upon, and welcomed in their individual being. See Holbrook, *Human Hope and the Death Instinct,* Part V: "Psychoanalysis and Existentialism."

16. For a presentation of the concept of the "true self," see Winnicott, *The Maturational Processes and the Facilitating Environment,* Ch. 12.

Chapter 5. THE BIRTH OF OTHERNESS

I originally delivered this paper as the first of the 1972 William James Lectures on Religious Experience at Harvard Divinity School. The lecture series considered the topic of religious experience in relation to the stages of human development as delineated by Erik Erikson, though the lecturers were in no way bound to use Erikson's theories as their only resource. We were invited to expand on religion in terms of human experience at various stages of psychological and physical growth. I was asked to give the first lecture on the first stage of human development, birth and the early years of the mother-child relationship. I discussed what the psychological dynamics of this stage implied for religious experience. Later the paper was published in *Religion in Life,* Vol. XLII, No. 3 (Autumn 1973).

1. Kierkegaard's stages of religious development are of particular interest to the contemporary psychotherapist because they delineate levels of psychological growth as well. Kierkegaard uses the vocabulary of the spirit to chart phases of psychological maturation. Today we do it just the other way around; psychological language is used to describe levels of spiritual growth. This exchange of vocabularies raises for our consideration not only the relation of spiritual and psychological categories, but also the significance of language as an indicator of change in the content of our experience, or at least in the style we find appropriate for its articulation. For example, what change is indicated in our experience of interiority if we talk about it in terms of the psyche rather than the soul? Are those the same? Are they different? Do the different words express a different relation to our inner life? Or should we treat psychological language as the means through which our late-twentieth-century culture tries to integrate the timeless religious mysteries?

2. See Helene Deutsch, *The Psychology of Women,* Vol. II (Grune & Stratton, 1945), p. 139, for a discussion of the identification of mother and child.

3. See Erik Erikson, *Childhood and Society* (W. W. Norton & Co., 1950), pp. 219–222.

4. Winnicott, "Anxiety Associated with Insecurity," in *Through Pae-diatrics to Psycho-Analysis: Collected Papers,* p. 99.

5. See Edith Weigert, "The Psychotherapy of the Affective Psychoses," in her *The Courage to Love,* pp. 146–149.

Chapter 6. THE AUTHORITY OF WOMEN

This chapter is based on remarks I originally delivered to a gathering of Episcopal women, among them candidates seeking ordination to the priesthood, in September 1975 at The College of Preachers and Teachers in Washington, D.C.

1. See Eric Partridge, *Origins: A Short Etymological Dictionary of Modern English* (Macmillan Co., 1958), and *The Concise Oxford Dictionary of Current English,* 5th ed. (Oxford: Clarendon Press, 1964).

2. For further discussion of this point, see Ann Belford Ulanov, *The Feminine,* pp. 355–361.

3. Such "inner images" are parallel on the personal and cultural levels to Melanie Klein's notion of introjected objects. See her *Love, Guilt, and Reparation: And Other Works, 1921–1945* (Delacorte Press, 1975), pp. 267–269, 335–341, 362–363, 405, 409, 412–419.

4. C. G. Jung, *Two Essays in Analytical Psychology,* p. 209.

5. The term "split animus" (along with "split anima") is one my husband and I have coined and found particularly useful to describe certain typical problems that afflict women (and men). After having used these terms for some time, we came across a brief mention of split animus in Robert Stein's *Incest and Human Love* (The Third Press, 1973), pp. 99–100.

6. This equating of others with the contents we have projected onto them is called "projective identification," a technical concept formulated by Melanie Klein; see her *Envy and Gratitude: And Other Works, 1946–1963* (Delacorte Press, 1975), pp. 68–69, 153–155. See also note 9 to Chapter 7, below.

7. See C. G. Jung, *Aion: Researchers Into the Phenomenology of the Self,* Collected Works, Vol. 9, Part II, tr. by R. F. C. Hull (Bollingen Series, XX; Pantheon Books, 1959), p. 33. See also Ann Belford Ulanov, *The Feminine,* pp. 35–36, 41–42, 50–51, 262–268, 270–274.

8. A variant of this pattern is found in women of real originality who develop their own views under the cover of explicating the theories of "the master." Melanie Klein, for example, persisted to the end of her rich career in saying she was merely extending Freud's views into an earlier phase of human development. In fact, however, she developed an entirely

new person-centered psychology in place of Freud's instinct theory. See Harry Guntrip, *Psychoanalytic Theory, Therapy, and the Self* (Basic Books, 1971). Lou Andreas-Salomé provides another instance of this phenomenon though to a lesser degree. Her original perceptions remain just that—illuminating perceptions; she does not construct them into a new point of view. See *The Freud Journal of Lou Andreas-Salomé*, tr. by Stanley A. Leavy (Basic Books, 1964). See also *Sigmund Freud and Lou Andreas-Salomé: Letters*, ed. by Ernst Pfeiffer, tr. by William and Elaine Robson-Scott (Harcourt Brace Jovanovich, 1972). For a stimulating presentation of the fascinating and talented women among Freud's early disciples, all of whom illustrate this phenomenon, see Paul Roazen, *Freud and His Followers* (Alfred A. Knopf, 1975), Ch. 9.

9. C. G. Jung, *The Visions Seminars*, Book 2, p. 451.

10. Ibid., p. 456.

11. See Valerie Saiving Goldstein, "The Human Situation: A Feminine Viewpoint," in *The Nature of Man in Theological and Psychological Perspective*, ed. by Simon Doniger (Harper & Row, 1962), pp. 151, 153, 165.

12. See C. G. Jung, *The Visions Seminars*, Book 2, p. 441.

13. See C. G. Jung, *Two Essays on Analytical Psychology*, p. 221.

14. Judith Hubback, a Jungian analyst in England, makes this interesting comment in her article "Reflections on the Psychology of Women" in *The Journal of Analytical Psychology*, Vol. 23, No. 2 (April 1978), p. 177: "During the analyses of many women I find a great anxiety is revealed about whether the twentieth-century enlargement of life and opportunities—on the face of it 'good'—is not bringing into play some deep danger which may threaten something which they know belongs intrinsically to them: and they are afraid of the attacking force in themselves."

15. What is needed here is the work of an "intercessory ego," which my husband and I discuss at length in *Religion and the Unconscious*, pp. 235–242.

16. See C. G. Jung, *Two Essays on Analytical Psychology*, p. 218.

17. For discussion of the symbolism of the Father archetype, see Ann Belford Ulanov, "The Search for Paternal Roots: Jungian Perspectives on Fathering," in Edward V. Stein (ed.), *Fathering: Fact or Fable?* (Abingdon Press, 1977), pp. 48–52.

18. C. G. Jung, *Mysterium Coniunctionis*, p. 183.

19. In his book *The Child* (tr. by Ralph Manheim; G. P. Putnam's Sons, 1973), Erich Neumann writes of "a masculine spirit specific to woman" (p. 97) as the spiritual aspect of the feminine: "This unconscious force is manifested in woman as a drive which compels and directs her

personality, but at the same time it is a spiritual content, a spiritual instinct which as image and intuition, as inspiring feeling or mood, or as a pressing need, guides and fructifies her" (p. 99). He continues: "These inner spiritual influences of the unconscious are manifested in woman as attitudes of faith and knowledge, as conceptions and values which often determine her life and existence independently of, if not in opposition to, her conscious beliefs" (p. 100). She is gradually instructed often through relation to a man in whom she experiences this principle embodied, but "the instruction does not take the form of logical knowledge; rather, it is the wisdom of Eros, which woman in her relatedness follows. In going the ways of Eros, she may be said not so much to fulfill herself as to realize the feminine spirit" (p. 101).

20. See Castillejo, *Knowing Woman*, pp. 86, 89.

Chapter 7. WOMAN RECEIVING

This chapter is based on a lecture entitled "A Matter of Presence" which I originally gave at Boston University, as part of a symposium on "The Future of Religion," April 1, 1976.

1. For extended discussion of the "intercessory ego," see Ann and Barry Ulanov, *Religion and the Unconscious*, pp. 231–242.
2. C. G. Jung, *The Visions Seminars*, Book 2, p. 478.
3. See Ann and Barry Ulanov, *Religion and the Unconscious*, pp. 26ff.
4. Magee, *Karl Popper*, p. 51.
5. See Ann Belford Ulanov, "The Witch Archetype," in *Quadrant* (Journal of the C. G. Jung Foundation for Analytical Psychology; New York), Vol. 10, No. 1 (Summer 1977), pp. 5–22.
6. Julian of Norwich, *The Revelations of Divine Love*, pp. 161–163, 171–174.
7. The problem posed for an infant by mass-designed care such as day-care centers or multiple baby-sitters comes from introjecting parts of many disparate objects which cannot provide a consistent object with which the nascent ego can identify. It is as if one were faced with trying to fit together pieces from too many different puzzles. We tend to forget how wide open our dependence on others initially is.
8. My own schedule as a teacher at Union Theological Seminary is a good illustration. With the birth of my son, I shifted two of my courses to the evening because I did not want to be away from my baby when he was awake. Though strenuous, because my long day now extended into the evening hours, this schedule was not as exhausting as carrying multiple guilts over neglect of a beloved child or a neglect of my teaching would

have been. Moreover, many students, especially those who needed to work to pay for their education, found this a better schedule for them. The cross-section of students in the courses took on more variety. We all seemed to benefit.

The second example comes from a colleague who owns his own business, and the woman he hired to run his main office. She was a maverick in personal style and in the hours she kept at work. He found, however, that she managed the work tasks very well and established a lively esprit de corps among the employees. Though she kept shorter hours than the usual 9-to-5 workday, she improved the quality of the company's work. He was more than satisfied.

9. Projective identification comprises a stage of identification that precedes symbol formation in a child's development. The child projects impulses, affects, and activities onto objects and identifies them with these parts of his or her own psychic life. The child does not then adequately perceive the reality of the object, and also experiences a great need to control the object in the role assigned to it through this investment of a portion of his or her own psychic life. Melanie Klein formulated the concept of projective identification in her investigation of young children, but it applies as well to adults. See Melanie Klein, "Notes on Some Schizoid Mechanisms (1946)," in *Envy and Gratitude and Other Works*. See also note 6 to Chapter 6, above.

10. See p. 34, above.

11. See p. 38, above.

12. See p. 48, above.

13. Julian of Norwich, *The Revelations of Divine Love*, p. 103.

14. See Cassirer, *Language and Myth*, pp. 62ff.